Jack LaLanne

PRIDE & DISCIPLINE

The Legacy of Jack LaLanne

In his own words and those he inspired

"Exercise is King, nutrition is Queen,
put them together and you've got a kingdom."

Contents

Acknowledgements

Elaine LaLanne All I wanted to do before I go to the next expression of my life, was to see that my husband, Jack LaLanne, got his fair due for his contributions to the world of fitness. Much of the younger generation has no idea what he did, or who he was. Hence, when Greg Justice approached me about writing a book about Jack's legacy, I was electrified! I had saved Jack's writings, articles, and would you believe, magazines that date back to 1934. Thank you, Greg Justice, for believing that this book needed to be recorded. If you hadn't asked, it never would have been written.

In the 35 years you have been a fitness expert, CEO, speaker, author, and book publisher, I am grateful for your expertise in getting this book out to the public. You are a one-person Orchestra! The many days, hours and minutes spent on not only your contributions to the book, but the time spent on Zoom interviews and Zoom meetings is deeply appreciated.

Thank you, Crystal Babb, Greg's assistant, for spending many, many hours on the phone with me rearranging, adding, and editing; frequently urging me to explain certain incidents in Jack's writings and to write a short story about them. While editing, hearing you read parts of the book to me, I think you could have another profession in voice over commercials! You are a delight to work with!

Deep gratitude goes to son, Danny, a top forensic photographer in Los Angeles in the last 40 years. Danny spent numerous hours ferreting out usable pictures, and many weeks putting together a timeline of Jack's life, which is in the back of the book. Along with Danny, I also want to say a great big thank you to his sister, Dr. Yvonne LaLanne and brother Jon LaLanne for their input, insight and always being there for me. Thank you to Jack's niece, Susan LaLanne, nephew Tom, and his son, personal trainer, Chris LaLanne for contributing to the family scrapbook. To our attorney, Edouard V. Rosa, for keeping us up-to-date on all our copyrights and trademarks since 1983. You have been a "Rock of Gibraltar" to me.

To all of you who either knew Jack, or were inspired by him, I am overflowing with thank you's for not only contributing to this book and to Jack's legacy, but what you have bestowed on the fitness industry. The touching intimate stories warmed my heart.

Deep gratitude goes out to the many people not represented here, but were enlivened by Jack! I consider you all a part of the Fitness Boom!

When asked the question many years ago. "What is the future of the Fitness Industry?" Jack answered, *"IT'S GOING TO EXPLODE!"* And EXPLODE it did!

If Jack were alive today, he would say to all of you, *"Thank you from the bottom of my athletic heart!"*

Greg Justice The world is a better place because of Jack LaLanne's mission "to help others help themselves feel better, look vigorous, and have an extended lifespan." He promoted living long through healthy lifestyle habits, by helping people to heal themselves.

Thank you, Elaine "Lala" LaLanne, for agreeing to write this book with me, and sharing Jack's writings (some of which have never been published before) with the world. Your energy and passion inspire me, and words alone cannot express my appreciation for you.

Thank you, Crystal Babb, for your help from start to finish. The book is better because of your participation.

I interviewed celebrities, world-class athletes, fitness professionals and everyday people for this book and Jack's legacy continues through "those he impacted." I would like to thank each and every one of you that shared your stories about Jack's influence on your lives and careers.

Last but not least, I want to thank YOU, the reader, for reading *Pride & Discipline: The Legacy of Jack LaLanne*. Through you, his legacy will continue to live on.

Foreword

by Lou Ferrigno

Jack LaLanne is the Godfather of Fitness, and a true icon of our industry. He was Mr. Everything. He was an entrepreneur, bodybuilder, TV host, and chiropractor, and he inspired millions of people all around the world to live healthier lives.

I first met Jack in 1976, shortly after I had moved to California. This was before I had signed a contract with Joe Weider, and before I was on TV, so I didn't have much money. I was eating at a restaurant, and the waitress came over and said, "Someone by the name of Jack paid for your dinner." I remember thinking how grateful I was, and then he started walking toward me. He introduced himself and, along with being shocked, I almost had tears in my eyes because he was one of my heroes growing up.

Jack was such a sincere person; he never said a bad word about anyone. He was always a giver, never a taker. He would always encourage and motivate people to do their best, and he always had such a positive attitude. When you were around him, that positive mentality would wear off on you, and it made people respond to what he was saying.

When Jack opened his first gym in 1936, doctors told him that lifting weights would cause people to have heart attacks, become muscle bound, lower their sex drive and cause all sorts of problems. Jack knew better, and kept spreading the message of fitness, nutrition and a positive attitude. He was the epitome of discipline and positive mindset.

Jack would say, "I can't die because it would wreck my image." But the truth is, his legacy will live on forever because of his vitality, positive attitude and wonderful sense of humor. It's an honor to be part of this tribute to Jack LaLanne, and I encourage you to remember another one of his memorable quotes, "Exercise is king, nutrition is queen, put them together and you've got a kingdom."

Lou Ferrigno
Bodybuilder, actor, IFBB Mr. America and two-time Mr. Universe

Preface

"People have to take responsibility for themselves and do something about it. They have to have *Pride and Discipline*. If you have these two elements, you won't fail in life's endeavors."

– Jack LaLanne

A Strong Desire to Live

(Jack's notes for an article on "The Will to Live," circa 2001)

If you don't plan your life correctly, you are not going to have a strong will to live. If you retire from life, nothing to look forward to, nothing to excite and thrill you, what is your desire for living? You should go through life with your blinders off, accept new ideas, be receptive to change; the only permanent thing in life is change. You are the only one that can change your life. Speaking of keeping yourself excited and thrilled, I can't tell you how thrilled and excited I am at this moment, as I write this to you. I feel in my heart that what I am telling you will act to motivate and stimulate you to do more and better things with your life. Keep up with what is happening in the world, especially the positive things and there are many. I'm convinced that right around the corner are the causes and cures for most of the killer diseases today. I'm also so convinced that most of the causes and cures will come from scientific, progressive exercise and a balance of natural, organic foods, accompanied by supplementation. These are the ideas I'm trying to bring to you and have you participate.

As a man thinketh, so is he. You have heard this so many times, but it is true. Think health, love, happiness, longevity and helping your fellow man - whoops, I mean person. You have to keep up with the times.

Introduction

Elaine LaLanne Have you ever been in a conversation when the name Jack LaLanne came up? The average baby boomer would probably respond, "I grew up with Jack and his dog. I watched him on *The Jack LaLanne Show*. He and Happy would do tricks for us if we would go get our Mom and Dad to watch."

The Gen-X folks would affirm, "Yeah, Jack sold that cool juicer my parents bought, and we made all kinds of juice concoctions."

What would the millennials and Gen-Z answer? In all probability, "Jack who?"

So, who was Jack LaLanne? As Tony Horton, of P90X fame stated, *"For the younger generation including trainers, coaches, and athletes, this book is going to really help teach them who he was and the impact that he had on our industry."*

If you work out at a gym, use a leg extension machine, any wall pulley machines, the Smith Machine or if the equipment has a weight selector, you can likely thank Jack LaLanne. If you use a stretch band, drink a protein drink, eat a nutrition bar, or even juice you can thank him, too.

Who Was Jack LaLanne?

Addicted to sugar and junk food as a child he was a weak, sick kid. From age 4 to 14 (1918 to 1928) he lived on his grandfather's sheep ranch in the Bakersfield area of California. Living on a ranch then was not like living on a ranch today. There was no indoor plumbing, water was pumped from a well, kerosene lamps were your light, and you took baths in an old galvanized tub. The winters were cold and often Jack slept behind an old pot belly stove. The family would go to church in a horse and buggy and to keep warm, his mother put hot potatoes in a blanket. She also made clothes from used flour sacks. Jack and his brother, Norman, who was six years older, attended school in a one-room schoolhouse where the teacher taught eight grades.

In the late 1920's, an epidemic of hoof and mouth disease hit the central California valley, and all the sheep on the ranch died or had to be put down. The family lost everything and moved back to Berkeley, California. Many times I've heard Jack say, "It was tough living that way, but I didn't know anything better. I learned two things that stuck with me my entire life, *Pride and Discipline!*"

After moving back to Berkeley, California, at age 14, Jack was so sick he had to drop out of school for six months. This was the period that his life was changed by five simple words, *"You can be born again."*

He opened the very first modern health club called Jack LaLanne's Physical Culture Studio in Oakland, California in 1936. He was ridiculed for charging money to exercise.

During World War II, he joined the Navy and was sent to war zones, GuadalCanal and Suva. As Jack stated in one of his writings but never published, "I was assigned to the ship, *S.S. Dashing Wave*, destined for the South Pacific, as a pharmacist's mate. What I was doing as a pharmacist's mate was beyond me. I had a Chiropractic degree but I had no pharmacology degree, nor did I have an interest in it. How the US Navy put body building, chiropractic and pharmaceuticals together I'll never figure out. How ironic! I no more than got on the ship and found out my job description was filling prescriptions. I immediately called my brother Norman, who was a Lt. Commander in the Navy and said, 'Norman, you gotta get me off this ship or I'm gonna wind up killing everyone!' So Norman had a chat with the pharmacist and said to him, 'You know that Jack LaLanne, your pharmacist's mate, doesn't know an aspirin from an enema, it will be a disaster if he remains on your ship.' Boom! I was off that ship and transferred to President Tyler! Little did I know that incident probably saved my life. I found out later that the ship was attacked and many perished."

Upon returning, Jack was stationed in Sun Valley, Idaho where he set up a gym and rehabilitated the wounded as they returned from active duty. As Jack put it, "They gave me this rec-room where they had a ping-pong table and a pool table, and put me in a little corner with a few barbells and dumbbells. The hospital in Sun Valley was loaded with the wounded and convalescents. The doctors pooh-poohed weight training. I pleaded, 'please give me a chance.' They finally relented because I was getting such good results with almost every guy who wanted to do it. So they took the pool table out, gave me this big space with seven civilian workers and I set up a gym like I had in Oakland with some of the same equipment. The doctors in charge wrote articles in the medical journals about this new, terrific, scientific approach, weight training for convalescents. My name was never mentioned. But anyway, the most important thing is that I got the message over to them about getting faster results with weight training."

Jack has never received the credit he deserves for his innovative rehabilitation efforts and I've dedicated the rest of my life to getting this message out.

Later in life, during an interview, Jack was asked, "Jack, do you believe you are leaving a legacy?" Jack, who had a fantastic sense of humor and not one to "toot his horn," laughed and answered, "Yesterday I was a crackpot, a nut, and a charlatan. Today I am an authority!"

How I Met Jack

In 1948, television in San Francisco was in its infancy. I was appearing daily on a 90-minute ABC variety show which included an orchestra not being used on radio. I was the co-host on *The Les Malloy Show*, and also booked the guests. I received a call one day from Betty Jo Brown, the manager of Jack LaLanne's Physical Culture Studio in Oakland. She said Jack LaLanne could do pushups through our 90-minute show. I booked him, and yes, he did pushups, nonstop, through the entire 90-minutes.

This led to his appearance on Art Baker's *You Asked for It* national TV show where he did 1033 pushups in 23 minutes, breaking a world record. Soon after, he was offered a 30-minute, five-day a week segment at 9:00 am, on KGO-TV, to do an exercise program. This was preceded by a kid show, called *Romper Room*. Eventually, *The Jack LaLanne Show* was syndicated, went nationwide and lasted 34 years.

If you haven't heard of Jack's TV show you may have heard of his feats of strength; such as swimming from Alcatraz Island in San Francisco to Fisherman's Wharf at the age of 60, handcuffed, ankles cuffed, and towing a 1000-pound boat. Or, at the age of 61 swimming the length of the Golden Gate Bridge, under water, pulling a 3000-pound boat. On his 70th birthday, fighting strong winds and currents, he pulled 70 boats, with 70 people handcuffed and shackled, a mile and a half in Long Beach Harbor. (Refer to the timeline in the back of the book for more feats of strength and photos.)

If you are using a stretch band for exercising, are you aware where that idea blossomed? Paul Bragg was at the house for dinner and brought a small round rubber tube. He asked Jack what he would do with that and in classic Jack style, he began twisting and pulling the rubber tube, and told Paul, "I can think of a lot of things I could do with this." In the 1950's Jack designed the Glamour Stretcher for women and the Easy Way for men with different tensions. They were made with handle loops on each end, a chart of exercises for the hips, thighs, waist, chest, posture, arms and hands, and an exercise record.

In those same years he came out with Jack Snax protein wafers, a protein drink, Instant Breakfast, a variety of vitamins and a Hi Protein nutrition bar. He even had whole wheat bread and crackers. He popularized the Jumping Jack, juicing, and supplementing with vitamins and minerals. In the beginning these ideas were all unheard of to his viewers. Coming up with new ideas, and selling what he believed in, was how he was able to stay on the air.

One thing is for certain, Jack was never lost for words, never deviated from his beliefs, and I never heard him speak about leaving a legacy. What he said then is what the authorities are saying today. He was very positive, charismatic, funny, patriotic and never sacrificed his principles for money. He was a great observer and loved the life around him. He chose to use what he saw and believed to encourage anyone who would listen. And I listened everyday to Jack state his mission: "I want to help people help themselves."

How do I know? I was there!

This book is not a biography. We want you to get to know Jack LaLanne. To that end we decided to put together a book of some of his published and unpublished writings that would give you inspiration, motivation, and insight into Jack. In addition, we want to share stories through transcripts, lectures, television pep talks, and Jack's off-the-cuff quips, in his own words and words from some of those he inspired.

Elaine LaLanne

Greg Justice Have you ever marveled at the course your life or business takes you? When you look back, can you see those defining moments?

I woke up one morning recently marveling at the course my life and business have taken me. A series of snapshot memories flooded my brain. On an early November morning in 1968 I saw Jack LaLanne's exercise show on TV while lying on the couch at my Aunt Ruth's house. I have such a vivid memory of that day, being kept home from school because of strep throat.

Jack LaLanne was larger than life and was called "The Godfather of Fitness." As a youngster his muscles, his abilities, and his fortitude mesmerized me. Our TV set allowed me to workout with him and to feel his encouragement like he was right there with me. Yes, he inspired me, along with millions of others. I picked up his gauntlet of challenges and pursued fitness as my daily way of life, fitness as my business, and fitness as my mission.

I related to Jack's struggles early in my career. He went against the grain with laser focus. He wasn't afraid to ruffle some feathers and to try new things. Jack liked to say, "Yesterday I was a crackpot and a nut. Today I am an authority." Much like Jack, I set my sights and plowed ahead.

It was Jack's inspiration, his lead, and his action that led to the development of the first modern health spa in 1936, the first nationally syndicated television show on exercise and nutrition, and the development of the leg extension, squat (now called the Smith machine) and weight selector machine. He also was the first to encourage athletes, women, the elderly, and physically challenged to train with weights. Jack's focused pursuit of purpose and his undying belief in the power of a strong body helped propel exercise science and natural health.

Autographed photo from Jack to Greg Justice on his 49th birthday.

For my 49th birthday (2009), I received an autographed picture with a lovely note from Jack. The note read, "To my friend Greg, Happy Birthday. Here's to 49 more birthdays. Healthfully, Jack LaLanne." I was touched that one of my mentors took the time to make my birthday a little more special. It was that moment that I set an intention to further his mission and legacy. I didn't know at the time how it would manifest, but through this book, with Elaine, I see it coming true.

I met Elaine LaLanne a few years ago, and became fast friends with "The First Lady of Fitness." Her warmth, spontaneity, and energy were as infectious as Jack's. Our joint mission, with this book, is to promote Jack's legacy to an entirely new generation. We're excited to introduce some of Jack's writings that were never published due to unforeseen circumstances, and it's very powerful material.

Jack's legacy is about changing people's lives through exercise, nutrition, attitude and faith. Elaine and I, along with all coaches and trainers, continue this legacy. The power we have to change people's lives is much more real and much more than simply training people to exercise. That power is held in a smile, a nod, a gentle push, a kick in the butt, a pat on the back, a simple "Let me show you," and a shared "Well done!" That is the power to propel and that power is held by each and every one of us. We learned that from Jack.

Jack grew into his legacy by doing and giving, and doing some more. He first had to find his passion and purpose and then he pursued them relentlessly, increasing his knowledge with a combination of schooling and practical action on himself. With every new success, he would strive for more.

He saw the lack of means and method, so he designed equipment to help people achieve their specific fitness goals. His weight selectors and cables are still in use today. He was the first to use chairs, water bottles filled with water, books, door knobs, door jams, and even walls to get people to exercise. Elaine shared a funny story with me about a viewer who sent a postcard saying, "*Jack, I've been working out with you for 10 years and that chair hasn't lost a pound!*"

His ideas evolved into bands and tubes which were more lightweight, affordable, and easy to use by the average person. Providing a means to achieve success, offering the encouragement to pursue that success, living that success by example, all with purpose and love. Isn't that what a legacy is all about?

Greg Justice

JACK'S PATH TO DISCIPLINE—IN HIS OWN WORDS

From the first breath that I ever took on this earth, I was a small, nervous, sickly child. By the time I was 4 years old, I had developed the worst eating habits that any person could possibly develop. My mother used to smother me with love because I was sick all the time. She used to reward me. She would reward me with cakes and pies, ice cream and all of those sweet types of foods. So, by the time I was 4 years old, I had developed this craving for sugar.

My whole life was sugar, sugar, sugar! It was affecting my mind! When I was in school I got failing grades. I dropped out of school when I was about 14 years old for six months because I was a troublemaker, and I was sick all of the time. It was during this time that one of our next-door neighbors, Mrs. Joy, told my mother about a man who would be lecturing about health, malnutrition, and exercise at the Oakland Women's City Club. My mother, being the sales lady she was, convinced me that we should go.

At that time I was about thirty pounds underweight. I had pimples and boils. I was wearing glasses and I didn't want anybody to see me! But we went to this lecture and the place was full to overflowing. We tried to come down to the front aisle to find a seat, but there were no seats available. My mother and I started to leave. I was pulling her. I wanted to get out of there. I was so embarrassed by the way I looked and the way I felt.

The lecturer saw us and said, "Lady with the little boy. We don't turn anyone away here. Ushers, put two more seats up here on the stage."

I'll never forget this if I live to be 150 years old (and I want you to stick around and find out!). They put two folding chairs up on the stage and there my mother and I sat. I was so embarrassed that I was perspiring. I thought all of those people were staring at me. Little did I know that they had as many problems as I did.

As the lecturer, Paul Bragg, continued, he made me think that I was a human "garbage can" and would say something that would change my life and save my life. His words planted a seed in my brain that would be there forever.

Paul Bragg (bottom) on Jack's TV show holding Jack in a handstand.

"My dear friends, it matters not what your present condition is. It matters not what your age is. If you obey nature's laws you can be born again."

Here I was, this young kid with a scrawny, sickly body and a fouled up mind, and this man said that I could change that. I believed it! He sold me a bill of goods. He was a strict vegetarian at the time. He told us about natural methods of proper eating and calisthenic exercises and all of the things that went along with them.

I went home that night with so much enthusiasm. I had to kick this sugar habit. That is what was controlling my life, that's what was destroying me. It was like hell on earth. I got on my knees and I actually said, "Dear God or somebody, I need help!" I didn't say make me Mr. America or make me a straight A student. I just said, "Please give me the will power to refrain from eating these foods that are destroying me."

And you know my prayers were answered because that night I went strictly vegetarian for seven years. I cut out all white flour and white sugar products. In five days time, as God is my judge, I was born again. I was like a different human being.

Now, if something saved your life, would you be enthusiastic about it? Of course you would! That's why I'm so enthusiastic about my profession. That was about 70 years ago and I'm more enthusiastic about my profession now than I ever have been in my whole life. The success that I have achieved can be attributed to one thing: believing in what I do and enjoying it. What made all of that possible? Discipline, discipline, discipline! To start out as a sick kid, begin working out--to make all of this work, it takes discipline.

My first introduction to weights was when I was about 15 years old. I joined the Berkeley YMCA where I was taking classes in wrestling. I discovered, by accident, that the YMCA had a box of weights. I had just finished wrestling and wandered into another room when I saw these two guys working with dumbbells. I wanted to work with them, too. They made fun of me and said, "Hey kid, if you can beat us in wrestling we'll let you work out with us." I pinned both of them and they handed over the key to a locked box in the corner of the gym where the weights were kept. I started lifting weights and began reading the bible of the medical profession, *Gray's Anatomy*. I became obsessed with it. It was my inspiration to learn the functions of the human body.

I became stronger and more muscular and more determined to get my message out. In 1930 at 128 pounds, I won the AAF (American Athletic Foundation) Wrestling Championship and in 1936 at 168 pounds. I won the AAU (American Athletic Union) metal for wrestling. I was

JACK LALANNE

put on the 1936 wrestling team to go to the Olympics in Germany but because I was charging money for exercise I was called a professional and taken off the team.

I entered bodybuilding contests in hopes to promote my desire to help people help themselves, a dream from which I never deviated. In high school, I developed a gymnasium in my backyard in Berkeley, California. It was complete with makeshift weights, climbing ropes, chinning bars, push-up and sit-up apparatus. School kids, firemen and policemen were my experimental models. I was taking pounds of fat off and adding muscle to them. I knew an education would be the key to everything, so I enrolled in Pre-Med courses, continued to study kinesiology, and earned a Chiropractic degree. I learned to develop muscles, strength and endurance. I wanted to build perfect bodies and didn't want to sacrifice strength for endurance. I wanted the body to be perfectly shaped and athletic at the same time. I also felt that proper nutrition was a big part of bodybuilding.

My dream of owning a professional gym was realized in 1936, just before my 22nd birthday. There were no fancy health clubs remotely akin to what we have today. Gyms were called sweat boxes. There were gym classes in schools and people like Paul Bragg toured the country speaking and holding calisthenics classes. Most people were not aware of the benefits of *systematic* exercise using weights. I opened the very first modern health spa, complete with plants, rugs, and glass tile showers. I bartered the work of carpenters, plumbers, electricians and a blacksmith in exchange for memberships in the Jack LaLanne Physical Culture Studio. I was considered a nut, a quack and a charlatan.

Although I had my pictures in BodyBuilding magazine's and my enthusiasm was high, no one was coming to my gym. The word was out that there was some muscle man charging money for exercise. I started massaging people in order to pay the $45 a month rent. One day I got a bright idea to go to the local high school and wear a tight t-shirt and talk to the kids. They taunted me by saying, "Let me see you touch your toes, comb your hair." (In those days, people thought lifting weights would cause you to become so muscle bound that you couldn't lift your hands over your head).

I would ask the fat kids how they would like to take off 15 pounds, or the skinny kids how they would like to build up some muscles. I went to their homes and talked to their parents. They were my first students. (Some of my first students, Dr. Norman Marks, 1949 Mr. California,

Jack at 19 -
best built man

Dr. Charles McCarl, Dr. Bill Parker and Russ Warner, infamous physique photographer, co-producer and announcer of my show, are in their 70s and 80s today and still working out.) Soon, the kids' fathers asked for an early morning workout. Mothers called for an afternoon appointment but didn't want me to tell anyone. Business boomed. I made personalized programs for each student. If they didn't show up, I'd call them. We were family. We loved and cared for each other.

I was charging $20 a month for memberships and I wanted to give my students their money's worth. To do this, I began to invent new exercise equipment to build up their enthusiasm. I would take my ideas to Paul Martin who was a blacksmith in Oakland, California. He would then make up a prototype. This is how the first leg extension machine, the first weight selector, the first calf, squat machine and pulley machines, plus many other pieces of equipment were born. Even my friend, Vic Tanny, who later opened a chain of gyms, along with some of my students who were opening their own gyms, ordered the machines. Eventually articles were written about this new modern gym. I still have the originals which I hope to someday donate to a museum. No, I never patented any of these ideas, and nowadays they are used all over the world. Paul Martin later made equipment for practically everyone who went into the gym business nationwide.

(some excerpts of the above were taken from "All Natural Muscular Magazine," June 1997)

Patricia Bragg Jack LaLanne reminded me so much of my father. After attending one of my fathers lectures when he was 15 years old, changing both his future and his overall health, Jack LaLanne transformed himself from being an unhealthy human into becoming a healthy powerhouse in a very short period of time. By the time Jack was 21 years old he had his own gym and a large following of students that included local police, firefighters and bay area community leaders. To attract attention to his message, Jack LaLanne performed various feats of strength during his career to show that getting older was a path to getting better which culminated on his 70th birthday in a one-mile swim towing 70 lifeboats with 70 people, one person in each boat!

No one has been more of an inspiration to people than Jack LaLanne. Not only was he dedicated to his profession and never deviated from his principles, but he was fun loving, had a witty sense of humor, great dancer, and a beautiful singing voice. His show ran for 34 years on television, turning his viewers into a healthier lifestyle. I believe it instigated an entire fitness revolution.

My father and I loved him very much. Elaine and I are still very close friends to this day. My father, Paul Bragg, would have been very proud to see how Jack LaLanne listened to his message and changed the world of health and fitness for the better! We were so proud to know him!

Patricia Bragg, ND, Ph.D
Health educator, author, lecturer.

SECTION ONE

Firsts, Feats of Strength & Awards

"Anything in life is possible and YOU can make it happen." – *Jack LaLanne*

Firsts

Jack LaLanne was a visionary and innovator. He was way ahead of his time and had a powerful plan for change in the future. He introduced new methods, ideas, and products into fitness. He was called a pioneer and trailblazer in the modern fitness movement, and is known as the Godfather of Fitness. Jack was a creative problem solver, strategic thinker, and had amazing leadership skills. He was also able to communicate his ideas to others in a passionate, caring manner. Jack never wasted time getting things done. Often, he would wake up in the middle of the night thinking about how a piece of equipment should work. He was so focused on helping people that he never got a patent for the exercise equipment he developed.

Below are some of Jack's most notable firsts.

- Opened the *first* modern health spa (Physical Culture studio) in 1936
- The *first* to have a coed health club
- The *first* to have a combination Health Food Bar and Gym
- The *first* to have a weight loss Instant Breakfast meal replacement drink in 1956

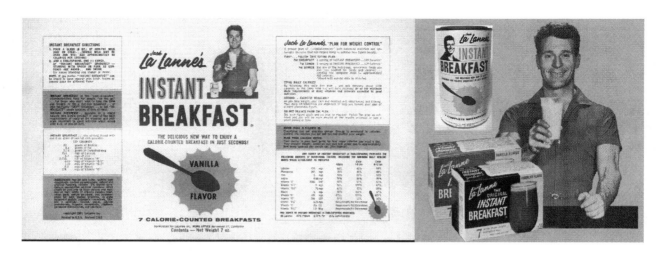

- The *first* to combine weight training with nutrition
- The *first* to have an edible snack nutrition bar
- Invented the *first* weight selector for cable machines
- Invented the *first* leg extension machine

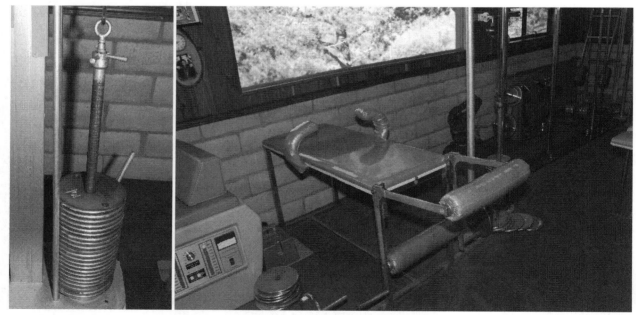

First weight selector (Left) First leg extension (Right)

Left and Center: Jack on the squat machine, now known at the Smith machine.
Right: Jack, at about age 28, using the first wall pulleys.

Jack invented the very first squat machine in the 1930s, which with new innovations by Jack's friend, Rudy Smith, evolved into the Smith machine. Below is Todd's Smith's account of the evolution of his dad's vision of what we now called the Smith machine.

Todd Smith Sometime in the early to mid-1950's, years after my father, Rudy Smith first met Jack at Muscle Beach, my father was visiting him at one of his gyms. At the time my father was a vice-president for Vic Tanny's Gyms. His sole interest was trying to improve on the types of exercise equipment that were available at that time. Paul Martin was the primary fitness equipment manufacturer on the west coast. While purchasing equipment for Vic's gym from Paul, my father brought him his idea of a more multi-purpose design of the squat machine. That's how the Smith machine was developed; it was an extension of Jack's original squat machine. My father and Jack never received any royalties from the machine. It was always about advancing the fitness industry. Several years ago, Elaine arranged for us to retrieve an original first generation squat machine that had been in the Norman Marks Gym

Rudy Smith & Jack

in Oakland since the early 1940s. After Norm Marks passed away, his daughters, Wendy and Rhonda, called Elaine and asked if she had any interest in the old equipment that was being placed in a warehouse for safe keeping. That first generation squat machine now sits in our offices in Las Vegas, and our family continues to be indebted to Jack and Elaine. Thank you, Jack and LaLa for such a wonderful history and that our family can be part of your legacy!

Todd Smith
CEO of Las Vegas Athletic Clubs and son of Rudy Smith

- The *first* to have a rubber stretcher (Glamour Stretcher) now known as resistance bands

- The *first* to teach scientific body building by changing the program every 2 to 3 weeks
- The *first* to have athletes working out with weights
- The *first* to have women working out with weights
- The *first* to have the elderly working out with weights
- The *first* to encourage the physically challenged to exercise and to work around their disabilities
- The *first* to sell vitamins and exercise equipment on television
- One of the *original* network television personalities and an original television pioneer
- The *first* to have a nationally syndicated exercise show on television

From Training in His Gym To Training on Television

In 1936, just before he turned 22, Jack opened the Jack LaLanne Physical Culture Studio in Oakland, California, the nation's first modern gym. He put plants everywhere and decorated the place adding saunas, steam baths, and other creations when he saw a need. Jack LaLanne's Physical Culture Studio was located on the third floor of an office building at 409 14th Street in downtown Oakland.

Jack's first product was Jack. He packaged himself in the way he dressed and carried himself. He enthusiastically introduced the components of his product one by one, his expertise in exercise progression, his supportive motivational elements, and his guidance needed to reach goals. He used his environment to help set the stage for this great product.

Jack was so determined to help people that his care and concern shone forth ever so brightly, and was evident everywhere he went (similar to a doctor's bedside manner) in what I like to call "treadside manner." He was so inclusive with his programming, working with athletes and non-athletes of all ages and abilities. In his physical culture studio, he worked with teenagers, men, women, to those in their 70's and 80's including the physically challenged. He made everyone feel like they were loved, and they basked in the attention and love they got from Jack. If they didn't show up for their workouts he would call them to get back into the gym, and he did this until the day he died. He had an innate sense of what each person wanted or needed to carry on, to commit, to succeed.

Jack's motto was, **"Exercise is king, nutrition is queen, put them together and you've got a kingdom."** Jack realized that the general population and athletes were not the greatest nutritionists. Athletes could accommodate a poor diet from time to time, but not the general population. Jack believed so strongly that exercise and nutrition go hand in hand, that he also included a health food store on the first floor of his gym.

As Elaine remembers: "One day while Jack and I were testing a new blender in the health food store, we put in juice, nonfat milk solids, wheat germ, nut powder, honey and a few other healthy ingredients, and blended it up. As we toasted, Jack quipped, 'This could be a great as an instant breakfast!' Right then, INSTANT BREAKFAST was born! The next day Jack approached a member of his gym, Mel Williamson, a biochemist, to create the first Instant Breakfast. It became a hit and had a good run in the San Francisco area and on his syndicated national television show. Around 1964 he sold his rights to Instant Breakfast to Foremost Dairies, as they were in a lawsuit with Carnation as to who owned the name. Jack then came out with a powdered protein product called REDUCE."

Jack also invented many of the fitness machines still in use today. Foundry weight plates were round with holes in the middle and different sizes and weights. They came in 5 and 10 pound plus increments.

Back then, there were no pulleys, or mechanisms to pull up the round weights with a round hole in the middle. No one had used a pulley to lift the foundry plates which led to the weight selector. Necessity was the mother of invention. Many creations came out of Jack's head, but being in his early 20s, he wasn't savvy enough to patent them. He was consistently inventing new pieces of equipment to keep his students interested in coming back to his gym. He also gave away free memberships to people who could help him. Jack Palmer, a pattern maker, was one such student. Jack would get an idea, draw it crudely on paper, and show it to Jack Palmer, who made patterns from Jack's crude drawings. These patterns were then presented to Paul Martin, a blacksmith at the time, who would hand-weld the first prototypes of the leg extension, squat machine (Smith machine), weight selector, wall pulleys and other equipment. Paul Martin later became a successful equipment manufacturer.

First Virtual Trainer

I hold an MA in HPER (exercise science) and have been in business for nearly four decades, beginning in 1986 when I founded Kansas City's original personal training center. Never did I consider training anyone outside of an in-person session. As many people are saying today that virtual training is "the next fitness revolution," the truth is Jack LaLanne was the original "virtual trainer" when he began *The Jack LaLanne Show* in 1951, before the jumpsuit, on KGO-TV in San Francisco (see picture).

His show was syndicated in 1959 on KTTV and ran until 1984. It was the longest running exercise program on TV until one of Jack's mentees, Gilad Janklowicz passed him in 2017.

Greg Justice

Transcript Of The First Nationwide Jack LaLanne Show (1959)

The Jack LaLanne Show was first performed for nationwide syndication in 1959 at KTTV in Los Angeles. Jack never used a script. He had in his mind an opening, a pep talk, and a close for every show. He did each show non-stop. Jack would film a 30-minute early morning live show, then often film 10 more shows the same day, taking short 10-minute breaks in between. Each show was 24 minutes long leaving room for commercials to fill a 30-minute television slot.

Below is the transcript of the first episode of *The Jack LaLanne Show* that aired on nationwide television.

Jack's Opening

Thanks very, very much for letting me come into your home. My name is Jack LaLanne and I'm here for one reason and one reason only--to show you how to feel better, look better, so you can live longer. Please keep your dial right where it is because I want to become real good friends with you.

There has been so much talk of late about the importance of exercise, the importance of better nutrition, the importance of positive thinking. All of these things we are going to learn together. I like to consider myself as your personal physical instructor and your health consultant coming into your home every day.

There's also many of you students who say, "Jack, I know, I know, I know that I need exercise, but, well, it's too boring, it isn't any fun, and I can't do it" or "I'm too old." These are all excuses, because I'm going to be here to show you how much fun and how easy it is to exercise. Well, I don't like to call it exercise, I like to call it Trimnastics. How much fun it really can be. And, I want to show you that you can do it. Does that make sense? Are you with me?

You know, students, you don't mind my calling you students, because I told you, I like to consider myself as your personal physical instructor, your health consultant. I'm so excited this morning, this being our first day together, me being in your home and you going along with me and having this fun. I'm so excited! What's going to happen is not what's going to happen to me, but what's going to happen to you. I have made up my mind that I am going to get you in the best condition that you've ever been in, in your entire life. I'm going to have you looking handsome, beautiful, and glamorous from your toes right to the end of your fingers. The only thing I'm asking you is to not miss one of these little sessions because I'm going to be with you every step of the way at this hour. And I sure appreciate your support.

Jack's Closing

If you appreciate what I'm doing coming into your home every day like this, just tell your friends about *The Jack LaLanne Show* on this station every day. Will you do that? Just send somebody a card or the telephone or when you go down and do your shopping, just tell them about our little get-together. We have to work this thing out together as a team. You're there, and I'm here. What a team we're gonna make, huh? You watch and see. Excited about it? Smile. Give me a big smile. That's the way.

Now that I have a date to come into your home every day, will you promise me something right now? That you'll stay with me for just five days? And if you're not more than satisfied with how you're gonna feel and what I'm gonna show you and gonna help you with, then forget about it. You can turn on a western or something else, some comic, you know? You can be entertained. I'm not here to entertain you, I'm here to help you. But I'm sure that you will be more than satisfied with the results you're gonna get.

I have been in this profession of nutrition and physical culture work for over 20 years. For the first 15 years of my life, I was not expected to live on several occasions. When I talk to you about aches and pains and about disease, well, I've really had my share of them. I know what it is to be sick. I know what it is to be well. I know that regardless of how out of condition you are or what your weight is, that you can actually be reborn again. I was reborn again when I started this profession of physical culture by eating properly and exercising a little bit every day. You can do the same thing.

I have learned so many fantastic, wonderful things. I'm gonna pass my secrets on to you. They're gonna be so easy to follow and make your life so worthwhile.

I want you to think of not how you are today, but I want you to picture in your mind what you're going to be. You know, I have never seen an ugly woman in my life. I really haven't, because I'm not looking at how she is right today, I'm looking at what she can be. So that's what I want you to do. If you have a few extra pounds around the tummy, if you're hanging and sagging and you don't have the pep and energy you should have, well, we're gonna work this thing out together.

I'm gonna show you how to normalize that weight of yours, how to firm yourself up, and how to regain and recapture that lost vigor, that enthusiasm, that zest and pep that you once had for living. I'm gonna show you how to get rid of those aches and pains because the only thing we're gonna do, students, we're going to assist nature.

As I told you, the facts and figures that I'm going to give you up here every day, they're proven. The reports are from the medical profession and all the top scientists. And believe me, if you want to start doing some 100% fabulous living, then let's be close friends.

Students, the good book says that our bodies are God's living temples. But how many tumble-down shacks do you see as you walk around on the streets? Plenty of them. People that are pretty much out of shape. If somebody gave me a wonderful present, like the good Lord who gave me this body, and when they don't keep the present in good condition, doesn't that show a lack of gratitude? Sure, it does.

Thanks very much for letting me come into your home. Don't forget to tell your friends about *The Jack LaLanne Show* on this station. Keep a big smile on your face, good cheer in your heart, because I'll be thinking of you where you are. I'll see you tomorrow at the same time. May the good Lord bless and keep you.

This picture is of Gordon Scott, one of Jack's avid physical culture students, who played Tarzan in the movies from 1955 through 1960. In 1955, promoting his first movie, *Tarzan's Hidden Jungle*, Gordon made an appearance on Jack's TV show. His trained monkey, co-star, lies quietly on the blanket while organist, June Melody, looks over the situation. Notice this picture shows Jack before he began wearing his signature jumpsuit.

A decade later, Gordon was training for the *Gladiator* movie in Rome, Italy. Son Danny remembers seeing Gordon at our home after a workout with Jack.

As Danny saw it, "Following Gordon's first workout with Jack, he exited our gym and had to walk about 50 yards over to the showers by our pool. Old Gordo was humped over with his arms hanging down as he walked to the shower looking much like the apes he befriended as Tarzan. In other words, he was "pooped" out!"

This picture was taken at KTTV in 1959 or 1960 during *The Jack LaLanne Show* about the time Jack went nationwide. It was often boring for the crew behind the cameras all day but Jack was so dedicated and believable that the crew started working out with him. Dave Bacal, the organist, is in the left hand corner of the picture. As there were no other exercise shows at the time, Jack hired Dave so that the music would follow him.

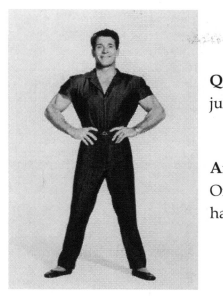
Classic Jack LaLanne pose.

Question: Why did Jack wear ballet slippers with his jumpsuit and where did he get his jumpsuit?

Answer: Acrobats and hand balancers wore ballet slippers. Only shoes available similar to today were tennis shoes. He had his jumpsuit made at the Oakland Pants Factory.

Denise Austin I was so fortunate to be on *The Jack LaLanne Show* for many years after meeting him in the early 1980s at the President's Council on Fitness in Washington, DC. After I became the fitness expert on the *Today* show, I would do a segment with fitness tips and information. I would always mention that Jack LaLanne gave me my first start on TV.

Jack would call me right up and say, "Denise, you're one of the only ones who always thanks me." I would credit him for my success and he would call me and thank me for remembering him. Jack was truly a **motivator**. So much of his legacy was his ability to motivate people. He was an **innovator** as he created so much of the equipment we use in the fitness industry today and he was the original fitness **influencer.** He was so far ahead of his time.

Denise Austin

AARP Fitness Ambassador, former member of the President's Council on Physical Fitness and Sports, helped launch the U.S. Department of Agriculture's food pyramid guidance system

Feats of Strength

"Your age is the sum total of your physical condition, the condition of your mind, and how you feel." – Jack LaLanne

Age 40 (1954) Swam the length of the San Francisco Golden Gate Bridge underwater with 140 pounds of equipment, including two air tanks; an undisputed world record.

To celebrate his 40th birthday, Jack swam under the Golden Gate Bridge under water with two heavy air tanks on his back. He started on the Marin County and ended up on the San Francisco side of the bridge with just breaths of air to spare.

Age 41 (1955) Swam handcuffed, from Alcatraz to Fisherman's Wharf in San Francisco, California.

Age 42 (1956) Set a world record of 1,033 pushups in 23 minutes on *You Asked for It,* a TV show with Art Baker.

Age 43 (1957) Swam the treacherous Golden Gate channel, towing a 2,500-pound cabin cruiser. This involved fighting the cold, swift ocean currents that made the 1-mile swim a 6 ½ mile test of strength and endurance.

Age 44 (1958) Maneuvered a paddleboard 30 miles, 9½ hours non-stop from Farallon Islands to the San Francisco shore.

Age 45 (1959) Completed 1,000 push ups and 1,000 chin-ups in 1 hour and 22 minutes. *"Happy"* is born and *The Jack LaLanne Show* goes nationwide.

Age 60 (1974) Swam from Alcatraz Island to Fisherman's Wharf for a second time handcuffed, shackled and towing a 1,000-pound boat.

Age 61 (1975) Swam the length of the Golden Gate Bridge, underwater, for a second time handcuffed, shackled and towing a 1,000-pound boat.

Age 62 (1976) Commemorating the "Spirit of '76," swam one mile in Long Beach Harbor, handcuffed, shackled and towing 13 boats containing 76 people. The 13 boats represented the original colonies.

Age 65 (1979) Towed 65 boats filled with 6,500-pounds of Louisiana Pacific wood pulp while handcuffed and shackled in Lake Ashinoko, near Tokyo, Japan.

Age 66 (1980) Towed 10 boats in North Miami, Florida filled with 77 people for over a mile in less than 1 hour.

Age 70 (1984) Handcuffed, shackled and fighting strong winds and currents, towed 70 boats with 70 people from the Queen's Way Bridge in the Long Beach Harbor to the Queen Mary, 1½ miles.

These yellow tanks were used during training sessions, but he did not use them during the actual swim. It was decided he would be fed a continuous supply of air from the boat to ensure he did not run out of air.

When asked what sport will be popular 100 years from now, Jack said; "Bodybuilding, muscle toning, physical self-improvement of physique. The Greeks were doing it centuries ago! Everyone now is getting more and more interested in looking better as well as improving physically."

For more information about Jack's Feats of Strength, including images, see the timeline in the back of the book.

Awards

Below are just a few of the numerous awards that Jack received through his career.

- President's Council on Physical Fitness and Sports Lifetime Achievement Award
- Academy of BodyBuilding and Fitness Award
- State of California Governor's Council on Physical Fitness Lifetime Achievement Award
- United States Sports Academy Dwight D. Eisenhower Fitness Award
- Spirit of Muscle Beach Award

- Inducted into The National Fitness Hall of Fame

- Arnold Classic Lifetime Achievement Award

- Interglobal International Infomercial Award

- Freddie, Medical Media Public Service Award

- Free Spirit honoree at Al Neuharth's Freedom Forum (Founder of USA Today)

- Received the Treasures of Los Angeles Award

- Muscle Beach Lifetime Achievement Award

- YMCA Impact Award

- IDEA Lifetime Achievement Award

- Doctor of Humanities Honorary degree from the Southern California University of Health Sciences

- People of Vision Award from the RP International

- Inducted into The World Acrobatics Society's Gallery of Acrobatic Legends

- Club Industry Lifetime Achievement Award 2003 at the IHRSA Conference

- Star on the Hollywood Boulevard Walk of Fame on his 88th Birthday

- At age 90 honored in a mass media blitz in New York, San Francisco, and Los Angeles. ESPN Classic ran a 24-hour marathon of the original Jack LaLanne Shows, and a Jack LaLanne Day was observed.

Kathie & Peter Davis We held the first **IDEA** Health & Fitness Conference in 1984. Three years later we created the Lifetime Achievement Award. No doubt, Jack LaLanne was to be the first recipient of that award. He represented the start of fitness and we felt that he would be the right one to give it to. He gave an acceptance speech that knocked our socks off. He picked me up on the stage and lifted me high up in the air. It didn't matter if Jack was on stage or if he was right in front of you, he was the greatest

Kathie and Peter Davis with Elaine

motivator and he always had incredible stories. Today, the IDEA Conference presents the Jack LaLanne Inspiration Award to a fitness professional who has inspired the world, which is presented by Elaine LaLanne. Jack's legacy is getting generations of people to understand how important exercise and nutrition are--the combination of the two and how intent he was on not just getting your body in shape, but what you're putting in your body.

Kathie & Peter Davis
Founders of IDEA Health & Fitness Association

Norm Cates No other name in the history of exercise even remotely compares to Jack LaLanne's name. He was, and in my opinion still is, the most famous name in the history of the exercise world, and even in the health club industry. No one else compares to Jack when it comes to the contributions he made to our profession. In the last 40 years I cherish the personal time I was able to spend with him, and his wife Elaine, which included his receiving the 2003 Club Industry Lifetime Achievement Award at the IHRSA Conference. Many more memorable times were spent with them at several IHRSA and Club Industry conventions and trade shows. Those of us who had personally known Jack know WHY he was so famous. He cared about people. His love for his viewers came through his lectures, live audience performances, amazing feats of physical strength and agility, and through the black and white TV sets across America where he instructed his audience on exercise and nutrition. The world is a much better place because of Jack LaLanne.

Norm Cates
Club Insider, Publisher and Tribal Leader Since 1993
First IHRSA President and Co-Founder, 1981
2001 Dale Dibble Distinguished Service Award Winner
2017 Club Industry Lifetime Achievement Award Winner
www.clubinsideronline.com

SECTION TWO

Mindset, Attitude, Visualization & Success

"Develop a positive attitude. Think, and picture how amazing you are going to be. Visualize it!" – Jack LaLanne

Your Mind Controls Your Body

In order to keep your mind active, you have to be active! I've known and proved for many years that the mind controls the body. What moves your finger, your foot or your arm? It's your mind! Anything you decide to do, starts right between your ears. Once you make that decision, know what you want and make a plan. Don't bite off more than you can chew. Plant your seed in your mind and water it with small goals. Don't quit when discouraged. Remember patience wins the race. Let no one make decisions for you. When you have those up and down periods, learn to work through them. That's where discipline comes in. That's where good health comes in. Sometimes you're more buoyant and sometimes down in the dumps. If you are reading negative things, seeing negative news, and hearing negative things from friends, it drags you down. It all comes down to disciplining yourself, what to think, what to eat, and what to read. Make sure you are getting enough exercise to wipe away mind cobwebs, so that you can become a champion of your mind and body. Learn a lesson from sports. No one becomes a champion until they take the time to learn and perfect their skills. Above all, believe in yourself! You make it happen!

Jack LaLanne, the flamboyant grandfather of the American fitness movement figured it his way, as he prepared to slip into the 60-degree water of Long Beach Harbor. If he could swim a mile at age 70, towing 70 boats with 70 people aboard with his hands and feet tied, there'd be no excuse for anyone to think they were too old to do anything.

Two hours and 25 minutes later, after battling a strong headwind that almost doubled his planned swim time and prompted some worry from his wife and friends, LaLanne emerged from the bay, feeling, you guessed it, younger than ever!

And full of homilies.

"The secret," he said, dripping wet and shivering, but his brown eyes still blazing, "is to believe in something and do the best you can."

"I believe everything in life is possible," he told hundreds of waiting friends, fans, and relatives, plus a couple dozen news reporters.

"If people don't have goals, they get old," as LaLanne kept the sermon going.

Daring tests of stamina are nothing new for LaLanne, as fans of the muscle bound septuagenarian know.

He marked his 65th birthday, for example, by towing 65 boats containing 6500 pounds of wood pulp across Lake Ashinoko in Japan.

But his overriding pitch was, "Don't sit around on your big fat behind, get up and do something," said American evangelist of flex.

Time and time again he was asked the same question, "Why?"

"Why does anybody do anything? You get the mind and the body working together, you can do anything", said LaLanne who began teaching people how to battle fat before Richard Simmons and Jane Fonda were born.

"Age is just a number," he added.

Mindset

Jack performed these incredible feats of strength and endurance because he *believed* that he could.

Carol Dweck explains the difference between a growth and fixed mindset in her bestselling book, "Mindset." People with a fixed mindset believe their qualities are fixed traits and therefore cannot change. People with a growth mindset have an underlying belief that their learning and intelligence can grow with time and experience.

Jack was a living example of a person with a growth mindset. He believed that all great things start with the proper mindset and attitude.

In an exclusive 1962 article for the *Saturday Evening Post*, Jack shared one of the "keys" to his successful life of continuing youthful vigor. He refers to it as "Mind Power--Plus" and describes it as "the power of the mind to direct the energies of the physical body in a positive manner"; "positive thoughts flowing forward."

It has been this "key" and others, successfully united in a disciplined manner, that have become the foundation of Jack's "Way of Life." Through Jack, millions of men and women have found a "way of life" from their daily progress of exercise, plus nutrition tips, as presented coast to coast on television.

Greg Justice

Excerpt from article by Dave Tuttle/Ironman Magazine December 1990

Dave: Jack is a firm believer in the power of the mind. To achieve your goals in bodybuilding (or anything else, for that matter), you need pride, confidence, and discipline. He feels that there would be fewer drug problems if people understood this. "Your body is your workhorse," he noted, "so make it work for you!"

"Pride in your abilities (but not conceit) is the first essential step. This leads to a confidence that you can establish your direction in life. Every day move in the direction you have chosen, and in time you will achieve your goals. "You need to plant a seed and let it grow," he explained. "Goal achievement leads to greater confidence, so you can take on even bigger challenges in life."

"Nothing comes easily. It takes discipline to make things happen. You simply have to decide that you won't do the things that are bad for you." Jack admitted that after all these years he still has cravings for sugar, but he asserted that "you can't give in to the cravings. You must have values. Life is not easy. It takes guts to live. Discipline is the difference between failure and success in life."

He also feels that discipline builds on itself. Once you have shown yourself that you can be disciplined, it becomes a matter of consciously deciding whether to give in to your urges. No one is forcing you to eat that candy bar. You set your goals and move with discipline and confidence toward them. Nothing can get in your way!

Bodybuilding is a lifestyle for Jack LaLanne. "Exercise," he noted, "builds the immune system and prevents heart disease, as well as improving your energy and sex drive. Bodybuilding is something you should continue for the rest of your life. Get hooked on building your body and never quit," he urged. "Be proud of your body. You can do the things you could when you were younger. Results are possible at any age. It's all in your mind. Exercise actually helps prevent aging. An active life and a good diet are the true Fountain of Youth. New goals and challenges will keep you young forever!"

"Your body is your most priceless possession, and the most pleasant thing in life is health. The true miracles are all inside of us, just waiting to happen. Nothing is impossible; focus on the events of today. Let's say you have 100 units of energy. If you spend 50 units worrying about tomorrow and 50 units preoccupied with what happened yesterday, what do you have left for today?"

"There is no secret to happiness and eternal youth," Jack concluded, "it's very simple, you can do anything if you want to. So, what are you waiting for?"

"The mind is a mine. It's full of diamonds. All you have to do is dig them up." – *Jack LaLanne*

Jack LaLanne's "Mind Power-Plus" Positive Thoughts Flowing Forward

1. Never look back. Yesterday is gone. Look ahead!
2. Plan each day with a goal to be achieved.
3. Recognize disappointment as challenges to make you stronger.
4. Be realistic in plans, but demand the best possible from yourself.
5. Be honest with yourself. Recognize the real you.
6. Always think young.
7. Always think physically fit.

You Are Your Attitude

Your attitudes are with you in every part of your daily communication. Your attitude is always there and evident, not just in any words that you might say, but also in the tone that you say them. Your attitude affects your hand gestures and facial cues, your posture along with the many things that are also nonverbal. Even if you attempt to carefully monitor what you say in any social or business interaction, your attitude will reflect outwardly in your behavior whether you are aware of it or not.

Now that you see there is a relationship between your attitude and your behavior, you may want to see how you have your own unique connections between them. Research has shown that people may not even be aware of their attitude or that they formed an attitude about a particular thing because of their existing beliefs. From where did you develop your attitude and how? As with everyone, there will be some of your own unique ways that you will want to improve your attitude as well as your interactions with others and the world.

Winston Churchill said that "attitude is a little thing that makes a big difference." This statement might be an answer to what has been asked by many and maybe even you have said, "Why do I do the things I know I should not do and why don't I do the things I know I should?"

Attitudes, as you are seeing here, are the power behind your behavior and actions. It is your attitudes that will influence you in everything you do, from what you choose to buy or eat to where you choose to live and how, even your job choices. Sometimes your behaviors turn out successful for you, other times not so successful. Research shows that you can modify and change attitudes you have that are a problem for your goals and desires, or even undesirable when you take stock of yourself.

If your attitude is wrong, you do wrong things, say wrong things, look wrong, feel wrong. On the other side of the coin, if your attitude is right, all will be right with you: your body, health, happiness, youthful looks and youthful feeling, vibrant health and vitality. What do attitudes do?

Attitudes Really Count

Yes, attitudes really count. I could write several books about attitude alone. What are attitudes? Look up in Webster's dictionary: "A way of thinking, acting or feeling. It can be negative or positive. Attitudes can either make you or break you."

In the field of sports, of which I know a little, we hear more and more about attitude. Take golf, of which I am a great authority! Why am I a great authority? Because golf has humiliated me, humbled me, and could, if I wasn't so stubborn, destroy me. I have participated in nearly every sport. If you're off your best performance you can recoup by trying harder. If I can do 25 chin ups and when I work out I only do 25, I can reach 50 by just trying harder. This goes with many sports: running, swimming, weight training, etc. But golf, baseball, basketball and most skill sports you can be off, try harder, and get worse. Why? This is what we call attitude. So many athletes in the above-mentioned sports were in slumps and overcame these slumps by what we refer to as attitude. By just changing your thinking from negative to positive. Again, as a man thinketh, so is he or so he plays, looks, feels, or performs.

The following story from Golf Pro Per Hanson, Bastad Country Club, Bastad, Sweden, illustrates the point of learning and playing with a good attitude.

"I met Jack in 1971 working at Lakeside Golf Club of Hollywood, established in 1924. Movie stars Bing Crosby and Bob Hope are some of the more famous members. Jack became a ball-o-holic, and loved to hit balls. I asked Jack many times after his Saturday morning game, "Did you have a good game?" He always said, "Yes." Most golfers I don't dare to ask if they had a good game. If they do, they always tell you anyway, hole by hole.

"Originally from Sweden, I came from The Country Club in Brookline, Mass for work at Lakeside, the home of the stars. Little after I met Jack he gave me a paper note to give to the manager at The Jack LaLanne Health Spas. When I handed that paper over, it opened doors. I became hooked in the gym and Jack saw my results and invited me to his morning show. I almost choked, and he said, "Don't worry. Just do after me. Easy enough.""

Jack and Elaine with Gary Player and Per Hanson.

When I was Invited by Jack to play golf with Gary Player, Elaine, Gary and Jack mostly talked about exercise. But on the 8th hole, I hit it 40 yards by Gary. And when figuring the distance to the pin on the green, he [Gary] asked me what club I was going to use. I said, "A 7 iron." He said, "I am going to hit a 1 iron, and when I get that check they are not going to ask me what club I used." He just drilled it to the pin and the rest is history. (A lesson well learned).

I do think of Jack every day. I have my own gym and never miss a workout. I want to be like him in my way."

Per Hanson
Golf Pro, Bastad Golfklubb, Bastad, Sweden

Aging Attitudes	Ageless Attitudes
I can't do it.	I believe. I can.
It's too hard.	Life is great. Another challenge.
It's not fun.	I'll make it fun.
It's too expensive.	You get what you pay for.
People will laugh at me.	People don't care.
I'm too old.	Age is a number.
I'm not very smart.	I'm capable and resourceful.
I'm not lucky.	Luck is skill with repetition.
Nothing good ever happens to me.	I'm the master of my fate.
Fate controls my life.	I control my destiny.
The world is rotten.	It's how you look at it.
I inherited it from my father.	I control my life. Anything is possible.

People ask me, "If I don't feel these positive attitudes, what can I do?" Often, an unfit person has a difficult time thinking beautiful, great thoughts and great attitudes. A fit healthy person has all positive attitudes, is easy, is fun, is challenging, and they believe anything in life is possible. You can conquer the world because you have mental, physical, and spiritual strength. This is one of the main reasons for this book, to help you develop all the great strength and energy it takes to make great attitudes happen.

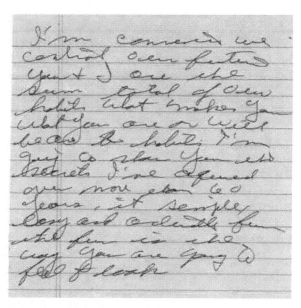

I'm convinced we control our future. You and I are the sum total of our habits. What makes you or will be, are habits. I'm going to show you the secrets I've acquired over more than 60 years. It's simple, easy and actually fun. The fun is the way you are going to feel and look.

Habits And Goals

Although many of us want to change a bad habit for good, we often say to ourselves, "I'll do it tomorrow." That tomorrow becomes another tomorrow and another tomorrow.

Find a *constructive alternative* to a bad habit and substitute the alternative habit for the bad one. It will generate healthy activity instead of laziness and inertia but, you have to have goals. I say goals because one big goal is often never achieved. Never set your goals too high. Set yourself an achievable goal and once you achieve your goal, set another then another. Write them down, see yourself as you want to be, keeping that achievable goal in mind day by day. It's rather like a game or climbing the rungs on a ladder. It's exciting and rewarding.

Overcoming Obstacles

I'm sure that you're like I am. You've had problems in life. Maybe you have problems right now. If you're overweight, underweight, weak, sick, tired and your attitude is that you are just plain dissatisfied with life, remember you can overcome these problems. If anyone is an example it is me.

I too have had to overcome obstacles. In my last year at Berkeley High School in California, I underwent a serious operation on my right knee as a result of a football injury. The doctor said I probably would never walk again. I was on crutches for months. As time went on I decided I was not only going to walk but also recover completely. I found the steepest hill in Berkeley and made up my mind that one day I would make it to the top. Each day I could walk a little farther than I did the day before, and after several months I finally made it that one-mile to the top. That was 1933.

During World War II, along with most of the men in the country, I wanted to join the service and tried, but I was 4F (unfit for military service) because I was unable to do a full squat. However, I kept trying to join some branch of the armed forces. My friend, Al Markstein, was enlisting in the Navy so I tagged along. As I was going through the line I did handstands, push-ups, and many of my hand-balancing tricks. As luck would have it, I wasn't asked to do the mandatory full squat and I was accepted. Another stroke of luck, the examining doctor was the surgeon who had operated on my knee.

At age 68, I was hit head-on in my car by a truck that went out of control. My good left knee went into the dashboard, and I had to have another operation. So you see, we all have defects of one kind or another.

My wife, Elaine, has also overcome injuries. One summer evening in 1973, while stopped at the stop sign as people were being ushered into the Hollywood Bowl by the Police Security, a bus lost its brakes on a hill behind her car and hit her from behind. The impact ruptured the gas tank and sent her skidding into traffic going into the Hollywood Bowl. She sustained a severe whiplash and as the bus bounced off her car it hit her a second time and wrenched her neck and right side. For years she was in pain but persisted in her exercises and therapy. Today at 77 she says she's going on 19.

None of us will be 20 again. Maybe we have stocky bodies, or extra long bodies, weak eyes, stubborn hair, big ears, or long noses. We needn't expect to be Venus or Adonis, but we can concentrate on making ourselves look attractive in mind and body. A woman or man in their eighties can't expect to look like they're in their 20's, but they can be a beautiful or handsome 80-year-old.

So if you're 20, 30, 50, 70, or even 90, I strongly feel that with a little attention, exercise, and proper diet you can feel youthful. Like the lecturer, Paul Bragg, said "you can be born again if you obey nature's laws". (Excerpt from "Revitalize Your Life" by Jack LaLanne).

Dare To Dream

After being so sickly for the first 15 years of my life, I began a program to rehabilitate my sick mind and body by setting goals for myself. Not long term goals but short-term goals. Remember your mind controls all. Move a finger or a toe, it has to come from the mind. You have to send a message to your trillions of cells that they are going to be better by your actions (proper exercise and better nutrition). If you send negative signals to your body you will get negative results. Send positive signals, you get positive results and a positive attitude. However, you must plant the right seeds.

I want you to have goals to dream about. The way I did it was to have a definite idea of what I wanted to look and feel like. It was on my mind constantly. I finally achieved all of my ideal measurements, surpassed them, set new goals, and continued to dream and fantasize about my coming improvements. I actually painted a picture in my mind of what I wanted to be. If I hadn't dared to dream, I would never have accomplished my goals. I followed this same procedure in 1936 when I opened my first Physical Culture studio and I used it in all my swims and feats of endurance.

Everyone has dreams and goals but do they follow through? That's the key. If you have a weight problem, you must count calories. We can't expect to supply our bodies with inferior food and extra calories and reach our goals. Too often, negative thoughts creep in and spoil our dreams. Negative thoughts like, "I'm too old," or "I can't lose weight," or "I hate to exercise," and so on. Wouldn't it be better to look on the positive side and say, "I'm lucky to live in America." "I'm talented." "I'm a good father." "I'm a good mother." "I'm going to accomplish my goals." Say to yourself, "Every day in every way I'm getting better and better." Remember you can't escape from yourself; you live with yourself 24 hours a day. Earn the right to be happy. It's not just something that comes out of the sky. Keep a good sense of humor. Laugh at yourself and at life experiences. Laughter and a sense of humor can make or break a person so far as happiness and success is concerned.

When you wake up in the morning, stretch, take some deep breaths and say, "I'm the world's luckiest person." Repeat the same thing when you go to bed at night. Feed your mind with positive seeds and keep daring to dream!

Arnold Schwarzenegger It doesn't matter where you go, there is a health club and it all started with Jack LaLanne. Jack had the first gymnasium, the first health club. Now, because of him, there are health clubs everywhere. Every hotel, YMCA, university, sports team (no matter what sport you do), every high school, every military base, every fire station and police station has a health club. And, it all started with Jack LaLanne.

To Jack LaLanne,

With appreciation and respect,

You my hero!
Best wishes
Your friend
Arnold

Arnold Schwarzenegger
Olympic Bodybuilder, Actor,
Former California Governor of California

A High Self-Esteem

If you have high self-esteem, you'll be healthy. Why? You'll have a positive attitude. You'll never be overweight and out of shape. You'll do things to make you feel and look better. You'll have pride in yourself. You'll have a great mental picture of self. You'll like yourself because you are doing great things to keep your self-esteem. You'll be honest, trustworthy, God-fearing, a good citizen, a good friend, parent, etc. High self-esteem means you'll be in control of your life. You'll have a balance of mental, physical and spiritual matters of life. This means you'll be eating proper foods, and thinking proper positive thoughts. You'll be physically active because the great law of nature is use it or lose it.

Motivation

Being motivated is a wonderful gift. It really is. As long as I can remember I was always passionate. I wanted to be a "somebody." I didn't know what, and I certainly didn't know how. My self-esteem was in the toilet, but even though I was an undersized skinny teenager, I would hyperventilate from the need to be successful, of use to the world. I was ready, willing and able, but my life was a daily struggle and nothing on the horizon held any promise. Not, that is, until I found the solution was in following a systematic program of exercise and proper nutrition.

Lack of Motivation

A lack of motivation is a hard nut to crack. If you slack down one day, you slack down the next day. We can approach the subject in a number of ways.

- The fear tactic. If you don't quit tobacco, eat healthier and exercise you'll get fat and have a stroke.

- The lost romance warning. How can you expect to find a decent partner in life if you don't even take care of yourself?

- Being overweight! When you have a great body, you not only have better health and fitness, but you feel special. Your friends compliment you and ask for your secret.

Of course, all these scenarios carry some truth but my usual suggestion is that the overweight person lacking motivation take some quiet time to themselves and find a full-length mirror. Lock the door and disrobe. That's right, strip off all your clothes. Don't smile and flex your shoulders. No sucking in that gut! Relax that tummy. Now stand sideways. Come on, let it all hang out. Now this is the real you. Happy?

Be self-critical. How could you let this happen to your body? You were born with the greatest gift of all: physical health. So why are you continuing to let it get away? This is the time to answer the question: Are you going to continue as you have, clogging your arteries, and adding layers of fat to every part of your body, risking ill health, aches and pains and an early grave? Or are you going to devote the rest of your life to being fit, feeling eternally great and eating only healthy nutrition that will not only keep you tight and lean, but will help you live for longer than the average person?

My Motivation

The greatest motivator of all for me was when I started weight training. I, of course, wanted instant results. The only thing that happened was that my muscles were sore. After squatting I could hardly walk. After bench pressing, my chest and arms ached for days. I had my doubts about the efficacy of lifting weights. Then after three weeks, I looked in my bathroom mirror and I saw bigger pectorals, triceps and even an improved V-taper in my back. My passion for, and belief in, weight training soared! Seeing progress is the greatest motivator of all.

You've heard the expression, we are all born equal. I don't believe this. We are all different. There is only one you, you can do many things that I can't do and I can do some things that you probably can't do. So find out what you are best at and what makes you happy and go for it.

Be truthful, especially to yourself. The only person you are accountable to is you. Be responsible for your actions, thoughts and deeds. Remember to be honest and true to yourself.

Motivation Mindset

- A new destination can lead to a new opportunity.

- Smile at trouble and grow through continuous effort.

- Imagine new possibilities.

- Aspire to climb higher and go further.

- The will to succeed outshines obstacles.

- Make time for a new point of view.

- It takes determination to accomplish the impossible.

How do I stay motivated? *IT'S EASY!! THINK OF THE RESULTS!*

Dan Isaacson Jack LaLanne is the **inspiration** of the fitness movement, a genius of **motivation**, and America's first **fitness teacher** through his nationally syndicated fitness and health television show. He referred to his audience as *students*, his constant companion dog was named *Happy* and he was blessed with his wife Elaine (LaLa) who became our First Lady of Fitness!

Jack is our fitness role model. He walked his talk and he always reflected the perfect fitness image in his appearance, actions and words he spoke! His memory continues to motivate us.

Dan Isaacson
Former director of California Governor's Council on Physical Fitness,
President of Isaacson Fitness, LLC, public speaker

Not Giving Up

When it comes time for your workout the devil will be on your shoulders giving you all kinds of excuses why you shouldn't work out! If you listen to that little devil, pretty soon you will quit the whole thing. So that's what I have done. I've developed this terrific discipline and this pride. I don't procrastinate when it comes time for my workout. If you don't believe it, ask my wife.

I 've been operated on a couple times with knee injuries. Even in the hospital, right after I got out of the anesthetic, I'd be there with weights. They would bring weights to me. I'd workout in or out of the hospital bed. I would work out around my injuries.

See, I've developed this conscience. If I would miss a workout, I would have a conscience you wouldn't believe. I want you to develop the same consciousness. I want you to develop this pride and this discipline. When it comes time for that workout, do it. Keep raising your sights higher as you go.

Maybe today you're going to start overhauling your eating habits. You don't have to do it all at once. Start eating more fresh fruits, more fresh vegetables. Start taking your vitamins. Start cutting down your calories. Eat more natural foods and when it comes time for that workout, make sure that you never miss it.

Anything in life is possible. If you don't succeed in life, in anything, you become a failure. Don't blame God. Don't blame the devil. Don't blame your wife, your boyfriend, your girlfriend, and don't blame the country. Blame you.

Take full responsibility for your actions, and if you do this, you'll have a life that nobody can exceed. A life full of fulfillment and of success, of happiness, and joy. You are doing something for the most important person on this earth which is you. If you are out of shape, you are sick, if you are mentally fouled up, if you are not productive, if you don't have love in your heart for your fellow man and your loved ones, what good are you?

But if you start eating right and you start exercising on a regular basis and keep it up, you'll have the greatest attitude of life that anybody could possibly have. Who is the recipient of all these great rewards I've been talking about? Maybe I'm redundant but the most important person in the world is you. Anything in life is possible and it's never too late.

Note from Elaine: Often when I would be talking to Jack about a book I was writing, or he was writing, I would write down a quote I could use later. Well, it's later. I wrote this down years ago, when he was talking about people being over the hill!

"Life is an uphill and downhill road full of curves, twists, and turns. That's why you have to keep focused on your destination. When you think you are in good shape and you get to the top of your hill, be careful not to slide down the other side at breakneck speed or a slow descent. Keep focused!"

Tamilee Webb Godfather. Pioneer. Inspiration. He had a good balance between his physical strength, his mental strength and his emotional strength. He was persistent. He did what he said he was going to do. I didn't realize until probably a couple of months ago what "abracadabra" means. Abracadabra is what you think and what you say you do. That was Jack. If Jack said, "I'm going to swim across the Pacific Ocean, and I'm going to pull this boat," he will do it because he knows physically he can, and he's got the mental and the emotional component to do that.

Tamilee Webb

Hall of Fame Fitness Instructor and creator of "Buns of Steel" fitness program series

Bill Pearl He was always so full of life and enthusiasm! An inspiration to me, and millions of people around the world. He brought the idea of exercise and fitness into homes and inspired generations to take better care of their bodies, through diet and exercise in order to get the most out of life. He never stopped encouraging. He will always be a legend in the fitness industry.

Bill Pearl

Professional bodybuilder, athlete, 5 time Mr. Universe winner, expert trainer, author

Visualizing

Elaine remembers, "I was always impressed with Jack's innate inclination for visualization. He actually visualized everything. For instance, when we bought property in a new area in California, intending to eventually move there, he visualized where his gym was going to be, where the pool was going to be and where every tree would be planted. Jack also visualized completing every feat that he accomplished and saw it as it already happened. It actually came to fruition. Jack strongly believed that the power of visualization is what can help make anyone successful."

In fact, one time in his life he visualized being an opera singer. I believe it all started between the ages of 4 and 14 when he was living on his grandfather's sheep ranch near Bakersfield, California. Below is an excerpt from one of his unpublished writings:

"Another chore of mine was to go down and get the cows every night so they could be milked. Animals became my friends because the two buddies I did have lived about a mile away. My brother didn't want to bother with me, as I was 6 years younger, so coming back with the cows, my imagination ran high. I pretended to have friends along the way and would talk to them. Many times I would stop and give them concerts. I loved classical music and would visualize and pretend I was a famous opera singer like Caruso, Tito Schipa and Chaplin, singing to packed houses and getting standing ovations. I wanted to become an opera singer. Later in life when I was about to open my Physical Culture Studio in Oakland California, a man by the name of Mr. Slaughter heard me sing. He wanted to pay all my expenses and give me a salary to study in New York for a year. In one way I wanted to do it to get money to pay for my studio but an attorney friend of mine, Mr. Segal, gave me a warning. He said, "Jack, you have a reputation as a physical fitness man. If you want to be a singer, do it on your own, don't be obligated to anybody." I took his advice and never forgot it! Singing became a leisure-time activity."

His leisure-time activity finally did come to fruition and brought him standing ovations. At the end of a lecture, I would put him on the spot, and ask the audience "how many people believe that Jack believes," and they all raised their hand. I then asked the audience if they wanted to hear Jack sing "I Believe" (circa 1953). The audience wasn't as enthusiastic at first, but after they heard him sing, a cappella, they immediately were on their feet with a standing ovation and clapping wildly. (and now you know how we got standing ovations!)

Jack's Thoughts On Visualization

To be a success in anything you first have to visualize your desires in your mind. For example, think of yourself as a piece of clay and now visualize how you want to look and begin to mold yourself to that ideal. I suggest that you find a picture of someone you admire. Put it up somewhere you can see it. This visualization helped me turn my life around after hearing a lecture from Paul Bragg. My ideal was K.V. Iyer, a brilliant Hindu physical culturist. He was known for his physical perfection rather than feats of strength and endurance. He was about my height and bone structure and, as a teenager, I wanted to equal his proportions. I tacked his photograph on the wall by my bed. His measurements were there in the photo. Next to it, I attached my own skinny, sorry measurements. One day, as will happen to you, I found I had suddenly duplicated my ideal and then some.

If you have fallen into a trap of no exercise and exceeding the feed limit, start fighting the problem with a positive approach. Learn to know yourself, to love yourself. Be cognizant of your future image constantly. When you feel like indulging in that extra desert, call up the mental image. Think of carrying that tote bag of fat around with you. Make short-term goals for yourself. A fitness program without goals is like a ship without a rudder. Set a course and follow it through. See the end result in your mind's eye. Remember the only thing constant in life is change. Try to change the measurements you have just taken, to your ideal. So if you are sick and tired of being sick and tired, start to control your destiny by getting rid of old concepts. Along with proper exercise, nutrition, better medical and personal body care, you will revitalize your life.

Jack Visualizes Alcatraz Swim

Elaine recollects, "When planning for his momentous achievements, Jack would visualize in his mind, mission accomplished. He would often say to me, 'I can see myself coming out of the water.'"

"After almost 20 years from the first Alcatraz swim, Jack announced to me that on his 60th birthday he was going to repeat the Alcatraz swim that he did 19 years earlier, at age 41. BUT, this time he was going to tow a 1000 pound boat--while handcuffed and ankles shackled!

"WHAT," I said, "you've gotta be nuts!" There were no ifs, ands, or buts. He was determined! That was it! He immediately started training. His training was a two-hour workout, one hour in the gym, one hour swimming in place in the pool, with a rope around his waist. My job was to go to the Ice House on La Brea in Hollywood and buy a 50 pound bag of ice. I poured the ice over him while he sat in the bath tub for an hour in his bathing suit. This was done so he could get acclimated to the cold water in San Francisco. I did this every day for a month, then he went to San Francisco to train for the next month."

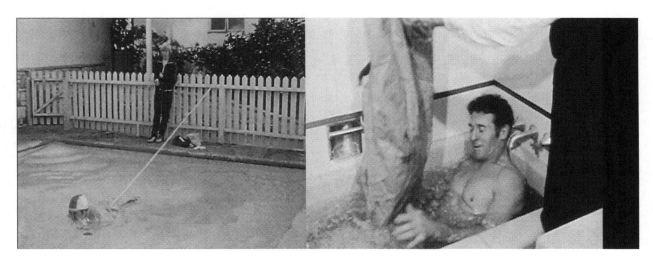

Jack Trains In San Francisco

Upon arrival in San Francisco, Jack didn't waste any time. After checking into the Huntington Hotel, the very next day, he worked out of the Dolphin Club, a Swimming and Boating Club next to Fisherman's Wharf that caters to open water swimming, rowing and 4-wall handball. (Jack was given a lifetime membership in 1954.)

That evening after his workout, he had dinner at one of our favorite french restaurants in San Francisco, called Alexis. As he was having dinner, he asked the waiter for some paper because he wanted to write some notes from his first day's training for his upcoming 60th birthday swim.

Below are Jack's original handwritten notes from that first night: six small pieces of paper documenting the results of his first day of training. As you will note, he was not a fan of cold water, but on page six of the small notepad, he began to visualize himself loving cold water and talked himself into it.

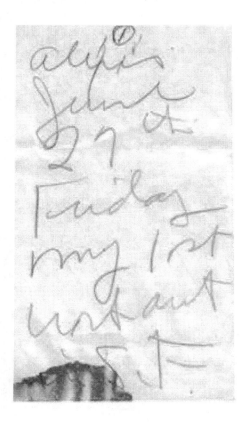

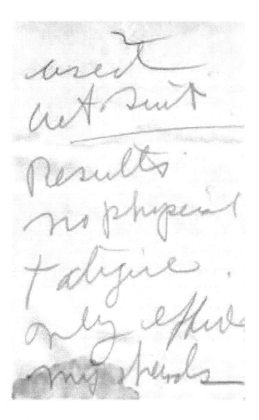

Page 1 "Alexis June 27th Friday. My first workout S.F."

Page 2 "Used wetsuit. Results, no physical fatigue, only affects my hands."

JACK LALANNE

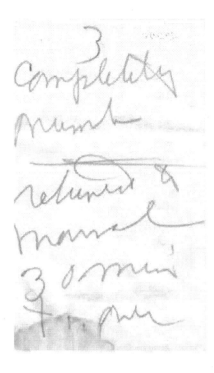

Page 3 "Completely numb - returned to normal 30 min +"

Page 4 "Cold water has never been a pleasure to me, but from now on, cold…"

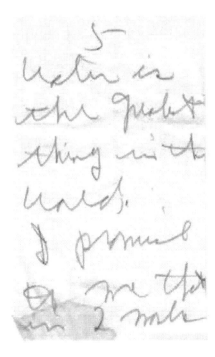

Page 5 "Cold water is the greatest thing in the world. I promise to me that in 2 months…"

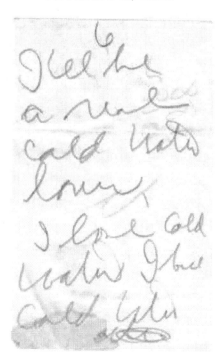

Page 6 "I'll be a real cold water lover. I love cold water. I love cold water."

The Huntington Hotel Stationery

Jack's second workout, after he returned from dinner, was written on the Huntington Hotel Stationary. He seemed to be more pleased with his training. He mentions Jerry Hawyluk who was one of the members of the Dolphin Club. Jerry, from the second day of training, rowed in a boat beside Jack, not only as Jack trained but throughout his actual feat. Having Jerry along for the training days was helpful as Jack got tangled up in seaweed during the first day's practice. Hence, the reason Jerry was in the boat.

Note 1: The 2nd workout at Dolphin Club was much more pleasant. No lasting numbness in hands was gone after shower. Jerry Hawryluk suggested swimming on my side to prevent bobbing up and down...action on side keeps me level with water... should increase my speed. I'm going to try to learn butterfly lower body action for better balance & more power.

Note 2: June 30. Worked out Sunday later in the evening very rough water, tide running very fast Really cold I was chilled, my neck legs and hands went numb took me quite some time to return to normal was chilled. 4 Monday morning 6 AM pulled boat for lst time Jerry Hawryluk.

Note 3: 4 continued... Weather good. Water fairly calm. I felt good no physical fatigue only coldness hands and feet went numb many distant cold water swimmers experience this I pulled boat probably ½ mile (30 min).

This was the beginning of his training in Jack's own words. Below you can see the outcome! Jack's visualization paid off!

Note 1

Note 2

Note 3

This has been acclaimed as the most unbelievable - phenomenal awe-inspiring physical fitness swimming endurance feat of all time.

MISSION ACCOMPLISHED!

Jack On Achieving Success

All successful people are achievers. What is success, anyway? To some people it is fame, to others it is wealth, security and even reputation. To me the first step to success is your health. That's your top priority. From there you can go to any of the others.

I've found that if you don't have your health and you're not feeling well, it permeates your mind; therefore your mind isn't as sharp as it should be.

Try this little finger test. Take the middle finger of your left hand and pull it back as far as you can with the force of your right hand. Now pull it back, harder. You're in pain, aren't you? Doesn't this prove that you can't separate the mind and the body? The mind and the body go hand-in-hand.

Achieving success then, means that a healthy body contains a healthy mind. A healthy mind sets goals. Achieving success means believing in yourself, being enthusiastic about what you believe in, live it, breathe it, dream it and give to your goals. As I said before, it's like putting money in the bank, the effort you put in you can take out. Dreams and goals are not reached in a day. Don't be a flash in the pan. Sometimes it takes years to achieve what you want, but don't ever give up. Remember the old expression, "If at first you don't succeed, try, try again."

Achievers are searchers, they persevere, and keep up on current events. A friend of mine weighed in at 200 pounds in June and later that year his weight was 160. Happy with his loss of 40 pounds, he wrote to me and said, "The whole secret of life is to know what you want, to write it down and then commit yourself to accomplish it." You can do it, too.

Some people think of success in a monetary way. To me, if you persevere, follow your goals and dreams; believe in what you are doing, the money will come. Some believe that you have to be famous to be successful. To me a famous person is one who is respected, loved and looked up to by others in any profession. When you are respected your influence will rub off on others.

Elaine recalls: Whether it be preparing for his TV show, a lecture, writing an article, or just saving a thought for future use, Jack would often write down his ideas on any piece of paper he could find. Below are three ideas I found in a written note for future lectures.

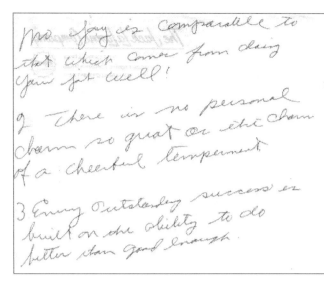

1. No joy is comparable to that which comes from doing your job well!

2. There is no personal charm so great as the charm of a cheerful temperament.

3. Every outstanding success is built on the ability to do better than good enough.

Brett Davis When I worked for Jack, he told me the two most important things are to always listen to people intently, because they really want to be heard and to keep what they tell you in confidence. He said if I remembered those two things I would always be successful in life. To this day, I still follow those two rules and it has helped me greatly.

Brett Davis
Personal Trainer, Clinical Nutritionist

10 Ways To Be A Success

To sum it up, never be satisfied, because when you are satisfied you quit growing. Strive to be the best in what you do whether it be a ditch digger or an accountant. You can be the best if you apply yourself and plant the right seeds. Don't be bored, because boredom is a villain in life. Always have a project to be completed. Make each day a new life, a new challenge, and you are going to climb another rung in the ladder of success.

I've said it before and I'll say it again, "Anything in life is possible if you make it happen."

1. Figure out what you want to be successful in. Studies, health, business, making money, friendship, school, sports.

2. You decide what *you want* to be successful in, not someone else. Being successful means hard work. If someone else decides what you want, you won't be satisfied. You are the one to decide what you want. Go get it.

3. Don't just stand by and expect success to happen. Everyday, in every way, do something to get you to your goal.

4. Draw a plan of what you want to accomplish. Be very definite. Everything you want, write out how you plan to go about it.

5. Patience wins the race. Don't be over-anxious. You can't be successful overnight.

6. Remember small changes lead to big changes. It's like planting seeds, you plant small seeds and they grow to be big living things. Don't bite off more than you can chew. If you want to lose weight, do it a pound at a time. If you want to save money, pennies grow into dollars.

7. Don't be a quitter! Quitters never succeed. Take pride in your stride. Learn from setbacks, don't make the same mistakes again. Use your experiences. They are great teachers.

8. When I was a boy building my body, I had goals. I would have these goals written out. I would have them where I would always see them. When I reached my goals, I'd change them to bigger and bigger challenges. I always had a goal to achieve. Keep the carrot in front of the horse. It makes life thrilling.

9. Believe. Believing is so important for success in life. I believe anything in life is possible if you make it happen. Ask that great power for help and guidance; so,

    a. Believe in yourself

    b. Believe in your plan for success

    c. Believe in the omnipotent power that is around us

10. I'm going to give you two words that if you use in your daily life anything will be possible. It can't fail. These two words will not let you down. Let them burn in your heart, soul and memory. What are these magic words? *Pride & Discipline.*

Pride. To be proud of who you are, what you stand for, proud of what you do, proud of your family, friends and country.

Discipline. This is what makes everything possible; when you say yes or no. Discipline. It controls your actions, decisions and thoughts.

SECTION THREE

Exercise & Nutrition

"Your health account is like your bank account. The more you put in the more you can take out." – LaLanne-ism

What Is Fitness?

Webster's dictionary describes fitness in several ways: "The state of being fitted; to be adjusted to the shape intended; to suit or be suitable; to be adapted; preparation." Like trying to define "love," it's impossible to come up with a definition that applies to everyone.

Fitness is more than just exercise and proper nutrition. It's a lifestyle, attitude and mental commitment. It is about today and tomorrow and creating that lifestyle for the future.

It's also waking up in the morning with no aches or pains, a song in your heart, and a smile on your face. You work all day and still have the energy to do the things your mind wants to, when you want to.

I believe fitness starts between your ears! It is a balance between the mind and the body. In ancient Greek and Roman times the great athletes were the great scholars. They believed that the mind and the body went hand in hand. I believe you can't separate the mind and the body, what affects one affects the other. The relationship between the soundness of the body and the activities of the mind is subtle and complex. Much is not yet understood. But we do know what the Greeks knew: that intelligence and skill can only function at the peak of their capacity when the body is healthy and strong; and hardy spirits and tough minds usually inhabit sound bodies." President John F. Kennedy once said, "Physical fitness is not only one of the most important keys to a healthy body, it is the basis of dynamic and creative intellectual activity."

"My workouts are a part of what I am." – LaLanne-ism

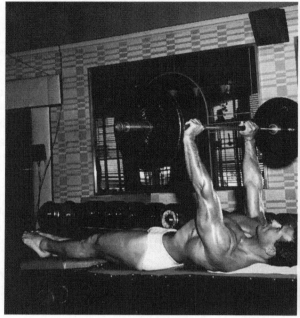 

Mark Wahlberg As someone who's constantly encouraging people to live a healthy lifestyle through working out and proper nutrition, I have the utmost respect for the man that started it all – Jack LaLanne. Jack was clearly a fitness visionary. His hard work and determination have been an inspiration to millions including myself. Though I was never fortunate enough to meet Jack while he was alive, I have had the pleasure of meeting his wife, Elaine, who is a bona fide health and wellness ambassador in her own right. Being spiritually and physically fit is the key to everything that has brought me success in my life. Jack figured that out long before I did. I can only hope that my words and actions can continue his tradition and inspire millions more.

Mark Wahlberg
Actor, Producer, Businessman

President's Council On Physical Fitness

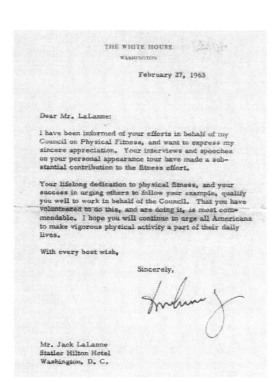

Elaine: On a snowy February 27, 1963, we were in Washington, D.C. to meet with President Kennedy to discuss Jack's involvement in the President's Council on Physical Fitness. While waiting in the office of the President, the Secretary approached us and stated the President had an emergency and couldn't meet, but Robert Kennedy was available and would see us. When we returned to the hotel, this letter from the President was waiting for Jack.

Arnold Schwarzenegger "After I became the chairman of the President's Council on Fitness, I called Jack and said 'I need your help.' He immediately jumped into action, traveling around the country promoting fitness. Not only was he generous with his time but he was a great leader, too. We have seen great leaders like Martin Luther King and Nelson Mandela and what people like Gorbachev did tearing down communism. We saw Sargent Shriver who started the Peace Corps and the Job Corps and Eunice Kennedy Shriver who started the Special Olympics. That is the kind of leader that Jack was. He led and he inspired millions of people to lead healthier lives."

Arnold Schwarzenegger
Olympic Bodybuilder, Actor, Former California Governor of California

"Life is like a game. We must train for the game of life. I train like I am training for the Olympics or for a Mr. America contest." – LaLanne-ism

Melissa Johnson By making fitness attainable and appealing through his long-running TV show, fitness centers, books, or public appearances, Jack was the face and force of fitness for many decades.

In 2007, when Jack was 92 years old, I was chairman of the President's Council on Physical Fitness and Sports. My team and I had the pleasure of honoring Jack with the Lifetime Achievement Award in Washington, D.C. When we announced his name and welcomed him to come up to receive his award, he gingerly got up out of his chair. He then started slowly walking to the podium, with his back hunched over and an unsteady gait, as might be expected from any nonagenarian.

Left to right Vice Chair Dot Richardson, Jack holding President's Lifetime Achievement Award, Melissa Johnson, President's Council Chair and John Burke.

After the first 10 steps, he suddenly straightened up, jumped in the air, did a couple jumping jacks, and ran the rest of the way to the podium. He delighted in tricking the crowd and showing us that he was still as spry as ever. Everyone was entertained as he received his award.

One of his main inspirations was his loving marriage to Lala. Jack and Lala were a dynamic duo and were very dedicated to each other. They both showed up at all our meetings and events, supporting each other, laughing at each others' jokes, and lighting up a room with their electrifying smiles. Lala is a big part of Jack's legacy of promoting health and fitness to the world. I think the global impact of Jack LaLanne could be its own super power!

Melissa Johnson, M.S.
Former Executive Director,
President's Council on Physical Fitness & Sports
and California Governor's Council on Physical Fitness & Sports

The Number One Law Of Nature Is Exercise

The only way you can hurt the body is inactivity. Physical fitness is not something you're just going to do for a few months or a few years. It is something you're going to do for the rest of your life. It becomes a lifestyle and it is not that difficult. If you can't take out a few minutes three to four times a week, whatever your goals are, then there is something wrong with you. I change my program completely every three to four weeks.

Everybody has time to take care of the most priceless possession that you have on this earth. Let me ask you this? How much would you sell your arm for? If someone offered you a million dollars for your arm would you sell it? Of course you wouldn't. You'd be a darn fool if you did. The most priceless possession you have is your body.

The Bible says we are fearfully and wonderfully made (Psalm 139:14). Do you think that man could ever make a calculator like your brain? Do you think that man could ever make a pumping system like your heart? Do you think that man could ever make a filtering system like your kidneys? Do you think that man could ever make a machine that the only way you hurt it is to not use it? Of course not!

Doctor's Okay

Get a physician's approval if you are new to exercise, if you are a smoker or if you're over 40. It is recommended that all men and women over 40 about to start an exercise program should visit their health professional and get a stress test that measures both aerobic and muscle condition. Chances are you will get the green light with a congratulatory handshake, but it's always best to be safe. Once you have the okay to workout you will feel on top of the world – ready, willing and able to train for the health, fitness and body shape of your desire.

Go Easy To Start

When helping newcomers to training, I insist they not take their exercise efforts to the limit. There has to be a degree of gentleness with your first few workouts. Resist the temptation to suddenly throw yourself into endless furious sessions of strenuous exercise. I want you to coax your muscles into shape, not pound them into a state where they are overtrained. Start slowly. After your first few weeks you will start feeling that you can push yourself harder, and at that time you will likely be ready to do so.

Excerpt from article by Steve Ramondi / Fitness Plus Magazine 1991

Steve: Would you advise someone to get back in shape if they have stopped exercising?

Jack: Absolutely. If you have once exercised, these are the reasons you should start again. Remember that when you take it upon yourself to start a program of exercise and you have laid off for a few years, you may lose a little bit, but you still retain most of what you gained when you exercised. You may lose 10, 15, or 20 percent but that comes back very rapidly when you start doing something about it.

Stretching

It's surprising how many people are into health, strength, and fitness but don't stretch. Ever watch a cat stretch? Instinctively cats test the tension, focus on the stretch and then relax. You too? Stretching is important. I always make it part of my workouts. Why? It warms up your muscles, preparing you for the workout to come. It also increases your range of motion. Above all stretching keeps you limber and flexible, two joys of life we tend to ignore until we suffer the consequences of no longer having them. Stretching also helps us keep any injuries to a minimum.

Your weight machine or freehand exercises are important for your strength and stamina development, but the flexibility that comes with stretching is priceless. It's your key to long-term independence and coordination.

We can begin to lose our flexibility as early as our 30's and it can worsen with each successive year, unless we work on our flexibility on a regular basis. We all have limitations of flexibility and I'm not suggesting aim for the range of motion associated with Cirque du Soleil performers, but don't disregard the added conditions, good health and feeling of satisfaction that comes with flexibility and improved range of motion.

When you stretch regularly you will:

- Warm up your muscles
- Increase flexibility and balance
- Reduce muscular tension
- Prepare yourself for exercise
- Increase the pleasure you get from everyday tasks
- Improve your circulation
- Increase coordination and agility
- Strengthen tendons, ligaments and muscles
- Improve your range of motion
- Enjoy occupations normally associated with youth
- Feel confident in the knowledge that you are supple, lithe and limber

The Breath Of Life: Breathing

Never inhale and exhale at the same time. That's my number one rule about breathing! Seriously though, if you think about it, breathing is our life giving force, without it we die. Breathing is the elixir of life. You can do without water for many days but you can't do without air for very long. Air is the secret of life. You have some 65 to 70 trillion cells in your body and they all need oxygen. When you breathe, you take in a wonderful life giving oxygen and give off the impurities (carbon dioxide). That's why it's so important to exercise. Many of you who have seen my television shows know that I advocate inhaling through the nose and exhaling through the mouth. Why? Almost everywhere we live today, it seems that our air is polluted with dust and smoke. When you inhale through your nose the little hairs in your nose act as a system that helps filter out some of the impurities you might take in.

As you age and don't exercise, your lung capacity shrinks and it's hard to take full breaths. Vigorous exercise helps keep your lungs from shrinking. Too many people just take shallow breaths in the upper chest. When you inhale let the diaphragm drop down. In other words breathe from your lower stomach. Try to breathe way down in your stomach and feel the air almost touching your back, then your lungs will fill with life giving oxygen. Your lungs are no different than any other organ in our body; if you don't use them you lose them. The more you exercise the more you breathe and the more efficient your lungs become. The air you take in nourishes every cell in your body and the more oxygen you take in the more it helps burn up fat. For instance, if you have a fire, the more air you put to it the faster it burns. The more oxygen we get in the body the faster it burns fat. So doesn't it stand to reason that if we exercise vigorously, we take in more oxygen, therefore burn fat faster?

Studies have shown that if people, as they age, remain active, they can maintain breathing capacities equal to those who are much younger. More important, is the fact that it's never too late to begin an exercise program and improve your breathing and physical well-being.

Sit down, take a deep breath in, and just focus on letting the air fill you up. After you've done this, exhale slowly through your mouth. Focus on a positive thought. Focus on what you want to achieve with an affirmation like, "success or confidence." Spend a few seconds focusing on your breathing, and while you are breathing, find your physical center of gravity, just a little below your waist. This part of your body centers, stabilizes, and grounds you. So when you feel stress, pressure, or head chatter, focusing on the feeling of your center will remind you of balance and control.

"The minute a muscle gets used to doing something, it's not challenged and does not respond! Muscles don't know anything. They have to be taught." – LaLanne-ism

How Much Weight? Live Young Forever (2006)

Whether you decide to workout at home or at a gym you must find the appropriate weight for each exercise. There is no way to know exactly which weight to use without a little trial and error. You never have to go for an all-out gut-bustin' strain. Your repetitions (the number of times you lift a weight) should range between 10 and 20. Your calves or abdominal muscles might respond better to reps in the range of 20 to 30. For most exercises, however, the best number of reps is around 12. This means you should use a weight that challenges you to get 12 reps. However, if you are new to working out, especially if you are on my side of 50, you should probably start with a weight that allows you to work up to 20 reps.

"First we inspire them, then we perspire them." – LaLanne-ism

The Scale Isn't The Only Answer

Men and women who exercise regularly don't depend on the bathroom scales. If you are not already aware of it, in density, muscle weighs more than fat. This means you can actually weigh more while losing fat because you are adding muscle at the same time your fat is burning off. You are exchanging lighter but bulkier puffy fat for denser, sleek, toned muscle tissue. You are on your way to a healthier, more attractive body. It's the mirror that counts. Don't always depend on just the scale.

How Often Should You Workout?

I have always trained. Even now I exercise regularly every day. I never miss a workout. Today many people spend their spare time watching TV from the soft surroundings of a bed or couch. This is an invitation to lethargy, and when they partner this laziness with eating junk food, they're practically inviting a heart attack in middle or later years.

My concept has always been to not sacrifice strength for endurance and vice versa. I am a great believer in balance. We have 640 muscles and they all need their share of work. This way, when you get in shape you'll have strength, endurance, and a well-proportioned body. My students perform cardiovascular exercises while working with weights. I allow very little rest between sets, a concept integral to my own workouts. I only rest 10 seconds between sets; in that way, I increase strength and endurance at the same time.

Change your exercise routine every two to three weeks. A muscle only responds when it is challenged beyond what it is used to doing. Changing the routine also helps to keep the muscles challenged. I'm also a staunch advocate of exercise programs that are of short duration. If the routine is too time consuming, you'll lose a lot of people. The program should be under 45 minutes for the average man and woman.

Training every other day is great, but you can also train two days on, one day off, or any other combination that works for you and results in at least three or four training sessions and at least one rest day per week. Generally speaking, you should exercise each body part from one to three times a week. Training a body part two or three times a week is not better than training once a week, but if you train each body part just once a week you should work those muscles harder, with more sets and possibly more weight. This way of training is not advised until you have been training regularly for a few months.

If you are a complete beginner to weight training I suggest you do only one set of 12 to 15 repetitions for each exercise to start, and work each body part two or three times a week. As you progress, you can add sets, increase weights, and reduce repetitions.

Another tip for gaining maximum results is to work the muscle or muscles to near fatigue. A word to the beginner: Make haste slowly! You must wait until you are in great shape before you can go full out and benefit without hurting yourself. When you get in shape, you will keep expecting greater results. Keep raising your goals. Remember, a goal needs a plan. And you need a plan for life.

"You can't compare free weights--barbells and dumbbells, with machines. Machines add variety but nothing is better than weights, especially dumbbells." - Jack LaLanne

How Much Should You Workout?

Don't have an hour to workout? That's okay – you do not have to perform an entire routine in one workout, although in earlier days when weight training was in its infancy weight trainers would literally train for hours. Now we understand it's okay to split the entire routine into two, three or even four sections throughout the week. How often you train and how much you do during each workout is up to you. I'm one who works out every day. You will have to arrange your family commitments, work, school and household chores to fit in with your workouts, or should I say your workouts should be arranged to fit in with your other commitments. The way life is these days you can be sure you will need to juggle some time, but make sure to slot in time for training.

"My workout is my obligation to life. It is my tranquilizer." – LaLanne-ism

Weights Are Great

As men and women get older several things happen and many of the worse things they experience come from a decrease in muscle tissue. They adopt a tendency to stoop and women especially may develop osteoporosis. Know this: Weight training will help keep your bones strong. Also, regular weight training guards against injury because resistance strengthens both muscles and tendons.

I have always professed there's nothing to be afraid of when you take up weight training. There are no undesirable side effects. Still, experts and critics shunned me for years. For example, many coaches thought if athlete's weight trained, they would get muscle bound. I had to sneak the gym keys to my pro athletes so they could train at night or 5:00 in the morning. Jackie Jensen, MLB right-fielder for Boston Red Sox, and 1958 American League Most Valuable Player (MVP), was one such athlete, and was strictly forbidden to work out at Jack LaLanne's. This had to be done in secret to avoid scrutiny from his coach, who thought weight training would inhibit player's performance and make athletes clumsy, stupid and muscle bound. At this time in my career,

Jackie Jensen with wife ZoeAnn Olsen, 1948 Silver and 1952 Bronze Olympic Springboard medalist being interviewed on *The Jack LaLanne Show*, circa 1950's.

business was improving and I moved to 17th & Franklin. One particular student of mine, Betty Joe Brown, was 100 pounds overweight and I helped her lose those pounds in less than a year and it completely changed her life. Betty wound up running my women's division. Weight Watchers had nothing on us. We weren't Weight Watchers, we were weight exterminators. This idea of weight lifting being detrimental to your health continued for several decades.

Today, it's been proven, you won't become muscle bound. You won't look like a Mack truck. Weight training is a healthy pursuit. Men will gain muscle, strength, and shape, plus lose flab. Women will also gain strength, tone up, develop beautiful form and shed excess fat. Vigorous exercise helps your mind function optimally and conditions you for other sports and activities. Your best life is ready to be lived.

Obey Nature's Laws

If you obey certain laws there are no limits to what you can do. If you want to be Mr. Universe or Miss America you've got to have a plan in your mind. You've got to figure out just what you want.

Whatever it is, set your goals and then make sure you go ahead and do them.

I work out early in the morning while most people are sleeping. For me to leave a hot bed and hot woman to go to the cold gym and work out takes DISCIPLINE! The discipline that you get from working out on a regular basis carries over into every facet of your life! You will become a better father, worker, citizen, and lover. Everything about you is better! I am convinced that the reason that America is so down mentally, morally, spiritually and financially is because people have lost their pride and discipline!

Your body is like a child. If you don't discipline that child, you have a problem on your hands. Your body is no different. Physical fitness should begin when children are in kindergarten. They should be taught what foods to eat and the importance of regular exercise and how it affects the brain. Kids could be much better students if they improve their eating habits and eat natural foods in their natural states as well as regular exercise. This is the most important thing.

When your mind says to you "jump," can you jump? When your mind says to you "run," can you run? Who's in charge, you or your body? You should be in charge.

Nature's Remedy

Exercise could almost be called nature's healing art. It has amazing powers. Exercise helps you increase your energy, it cleans out your arteries, improves your posture, increases your mobility, adds muscle and tone, improves strength, builds confidence, burns fat, strengthens bones, improves metabolism, augments your flexibility, strengthens your immune system, and shapes your body like nothing else in the world. You become a more attractive person in every way when you exercise regularly. Even your arteries will thank you.

Exercise has been my savior. It has kept me free of disease and made me feel on top of the world ever since I adopted it in my teens. Sometimes you may feel too tired to exercise. We all have moments like that, especially after a long day at the office. Obviously if we are genuinely ill or exhausted then we might have to miss a planned workout, but in most cases one's "tiredness" is little more than a temporary situation - and one that can be immediately

Jack exercising at 95 years old

changed with a little exercise. Drag yourself to the gym or wherever you exercise and start on something simple. Soon, as your blood starts to circulate, you will be rarin' to go for a full-scale, all-out workout. It has helped me to reach 95 years of age.

As people get older and slack off on exercise and nutrition they find they can't do the things they used to do, such as walk or run as fast, dance as long, or stay up as late. Now that's where fitness comes in. You can improve your strength, endurance, reflexes and your overall condition by exchanging a few bad habits for a few good habits. When this is accomplished your self-esteem goes up, your immune system is better, and you can cope with emergencies more readily because you have the reserve energy to recoup faster.

Good Health And Intellect--Two Blessings In Life

I see scientific and medical progress taking place all around me. But sometimes I wonder how we are doing as human beings. When I take a long hard look around me, I am not impressed. A recent fact was brought to my attention. It was that children today are not expected to live for as long as their parents. Kind of sad, isn't it? Statistically this means that kids, because of their inactive lifestyles and poor eating habits, will not live to the age their parents will likely live. Of course, there will be exceptions, but the point is clear. Good health and good intellect are the two greatest blessings in life. If you are born with health, as most of us are, you have hope. And if you have hope you have everything. Without health, where is the joy in life? Too many people are unaware in matters of health, fitness, exercise and nutrition and it is reaching tremendous proportions. And look how many people try to make money from it. Check out any drug store and look at the scores of products that are supposed to help us eliminate better, beat stomach aches, relieve heartburn, stop diarrhea, cure headaches, lose weight, overcome skin problems, varicose veins, bad breath, hypertension and fatigue. You name it.

Americans spend billions upon billions of dollars on tobacco, booze, and junk food, and then spend billions more on drugs. There is no doubt that millions of men and women are living far below their best level of physical fitness. We are all in agreement that our health is important, yet health is not valued until sickness comes. Many doctors agree with me that most of the causes of dying before one's time are avoidable, ignorant and careless about our wellness factor.

You Are Unique

Being fit is unique to each of us because each of us is unique in this great universe. Just as there are no two grains of sand alike or two leaves alike, so it is with us, there are no two bodies alike. Everyone is capable of achieving a level of fitness that is right for that person. You, and you alone, are responsible for your fitness, no one else can do it for you. However, you must want to become fit. We go through this life only once and we have only one body to take with us, so let's make the best of it. Everyone would do well to run a personal check on what he or she is doing to promote fitness. Am I getting enough rest? Am I eating the right foods? Do I have a hobby that really relieves the nervous pressures of my life? Am I exercising and building reserves of energy I need for true fitness?

When we take care of our body it takes care of us, both physically and mentally. A fit body makes us feel better and look better; it makes us have more pride and discipline in ourselves.

Make Out A Program

One of my golden rules for complete fitness is; make out a program of exercise that fits your needs. Work out vigorously at least three or four times a week at home or in a gym, and on the other days do some stretching and/or fast walking. Do something every day so that you will rise above temptation and won't let yourself get out of the exercise habit. You eat every day, you sleep every day, you brush your teeth every day. Your body was made to move. You should do some form of movement every day. Change your program every two to three weeks because when a muscle gets

JACK LALANNE
Creator of Exercise for Fifty Years

Since the mid 1930's, Jack LaLanne has been developing various types of exercise routines. Many of the exercise movements used as standard ways to improve physical fitness were created by America's number one physical fitness authority, Jack LaLanne.

The following is a list of some of Jack's exercises:

The Exterminator – helps firm up the entire body
The Fighter – a punching exercise
Stretchnastics – LaLanne stretching moves
Fannie Firmer – helps firm buttocks
Jumping Jacks – cardiovascular warm-up
Backwards Leg Extensions – single leg tucks and extensions
Posture Improver – pretend to try and crack a walnut between your buttocks
Rockette Kicker – overhead kicks
Get up and Get down – lie on the floor, get up, lie down, and repeat several times
Lower Body Firmer – leg scissors, lying on your side
Towel Breaker – series of exercises using a towel
Broom Stick – series of exercises using a broomstick
Chair – LaLanne chair routines, made famous by Jack on TV

Others are the Pincher, the Killer, the Face Saver, the Eradicator, the Rotator, the Lifter, the Eraser, the Fat Burner, the Gut Buster, the Waist Away, the Gooser, and the TensionFighter, just to name a few.

used to doing the same thing it isn't challenged anymore. A muscle needs to be challenged to improve. Make exercise a habit for the rest of your life.

When I pioneered physical fitness with my daily TV shows, I received thousands and thousands of thank-you letters. I shouldn't have been thanked. My viewers should have thanked themselves because they are the ones who did the work. All I did was give them the tools. The point is, don't just sit there, do something! Fitness is the maximum you!

"EXERCISE! Your health account and your bank account, they're the same thing. The more you put in, the more you can take out." – LaLanne-ism

BASIC EXERCISES FOR KEEPING FIT

1. **DYNAMIC SWING (Warm-up Exercise)**
Stand erect, feet apart width of shoulders. Clasp both hands together. Swing forward, bending at waist with knees bent slightly. Extend hands between legs as far as possible; return to original position. Inhale coming up and exhale going down. Repeat at least 5 times and work up to more each day.

2. **SHOULDERS & UPPER BACK**
Stand erect. Hold book in each hand as pictured. Press arms overhead, close to ears, lifting them up and down. Repeat 5-10 times - establish a goal; try to do a little more each day.

3. **CHEST AND/OR BUSTLINE- BACK OF ARMS**
Place hands on chair or bench as pictured. Keep elbows wide, legs straight and spread apart. Try to touch head to seat of chair. Return to original position. Repeat as many times WITHOUT STRAINING -- do more each day.

4. **WAISTLINE**
Assume sitting position on edge of chair, legs straight out. Curl knees tightly to chest. Assume position 2 and return to original - repeat 3-5 times. Rest for a few seconds, take a deep breath and repeat.

5. **ALTERNATE LEG RAISES**
(This exercise is designed for those unable to raise both legs to chest.) ADDITIONAL EXERCISE FOR WAIST. Lift right leg as high as possible and then repeat with left leg. Continue, alternating legs without straining.
NOTE: Use 1st position in No. 4 Exercise for this exercise.

6. **LEG EXTENSIONS TO BACK**
(For lower back, hips, back of legs and back of neck.)
Place hands on chair with arms straight -- DO NOT BEND. Raise right leg high, then raise left leg. Keep straight, pointed toes. Alternate legs quickly at first then hold position for a few seconds as you have each leg in air. Do at least 10 repetitions for each leg at first. Then work up to more.

7. **SIDE-BENDS**
(Note: Book weight creates resistance, which brings faster results).
Assume 1st position with book in left hand and press right hand against side of head. Now bend to left as far as possible. Do the same thing for right side; left hand to head, with book in right. Repeat several times, depending on your capabilities.
(Great exercise when watching T.V.)

8. **HIPS AND THIGHS**
Sit on edge of chair, knees and feet together. Stand up, then sit down. DO NOT USE ARMS FOR ASSISTANCE, UNLESS NECESSARY. Repeat 10 times or more, always keeping chest and stomach in.

9. **TOE RAISES**
(For legs, ankles and feet)
Stand behind chair for balance with balls of feet resting on book -- heels off. Hold waist in, keep head up and hips forward. Raise up on toes, as high as you can, then drop heels to floor. Heels are together. FOR VARIATION - do same exercise turning toes out, heels together; also vary with toes pointed in, heels out. Repeat 5-10 times.

10. **RUNNING-IN-PLACE/OR MARCHING-IN-PLACE**
(Cardo-vascular respiratory conditioner)
Run in place or trot from room to room; get blood stirring. Start running 5 seconds each day, but do ONLY what you are able. Stop, rest, fill-up those lungs -- breath deeply. The higher knees are raised the better.
NOTE: Be sure and check with your Physician before doing this exercise (i.e. stress test).

IMPORTANT NOTE:
The above exercises are recommended for everyone, however, please consult your physician for your individual needs.

The above images are from the flyer that Jack would hand out to his lecture participants.

Hydronastics

Water has always held a tremendous fascination for me. When I was a small boy, I lived in Bakersfield, CA on a sheep ranch. Anyone who has ever been in Bakersfield knows the unbearable summers. The heat is suffocating and it was a relief to swim in the irrigation canal. I'll never forget how I learned to swim--my older brother, Norman, could swim and he and his buddies had a favorite swimming hole. They took me down and promised me they would teach me to swim. They sure did, by throwing me in the middle of the big hole, fully clothed, and said 'sink or swim'. Well, I didn't sink and I've been swimming ever since.

Throughout history, water has been known for its curative properties. I was indoctrinated very early in life about the therapeutic value of hydrotherapy. My mother, Jennie's religion, was Seventh Day Adventist; they were big advocates of the values of hot and cold treatment. Any time any one would become ill or receive injuries, the treatment would often be hot and cold therapy, always with miraculous results. It all became very clear to me that they were increasing circulation. The hot, dilating the blood vessels and cold, constricting the blood vessels, therefore increasing the blood supply to the affected spot. This resulted in helping with rehabilitation.

If I received any injuries I would always work them out in the water. Personally, I found by swimming in the chilly water in San Francisco I felt invigorated. When I would advocate and recommend water therapy not only to my athlete friends but my students, they were pleasantly surprised at the fast results. When I first became curious about water exercises, I had my first knee operation from a football injury. In those days, knee operations were very serious and not too successful. I found the buoyancy of the water took the strain off the injured part. I was more and more convinced that water exercises, or as I call them hyrdronastics, should be added into my teaching. So I took it upon myself to devise a bodybuilding and conditioning program in the water. I used all my knowledge of kinesiology and myology to devise a program of Jack LaLanne Hydronastics.

Jack LaLanne's Hydronastics:
Fountain of Youth Exercises

Always check with your physician before beginning any exercise program. Water gives you resistance. When doing water exercises, at all times, lift water do not try to kick it. Make haste slowly. Begin with 2 or 3 repetitions of each exercise and try to work your way up to 10 repetitions. Do

Lower Body Water Exercises:

1) **Windmill Warm-up**: Arms straight, fingers extended, hands together under water. Pull and push water, first to the right, then to the left. Benefits the sides of the waist and midsection.

2) **Punching**: Elbows close to side, fists closed, knees bent, feet shoulder width apart, alternate punches under water. First punch water straight out, then turn and punch to the left and then to the right. Helps tone chest, shoulders and arms.

3) **Face Down Leg Lifts**: Holding onto edge of pool, face down, arms straight, legs straight, lift legs up and down trying to touch the bottom of the pool. Pull up with the right and pull down with the left. Helps tone waist, hips, buttocks, back and front of legs. In fact, most muscles in the lower body except the calves.

4) **Face Up Leg Lifts**: Holding onto the edge of the pool, face up, legs straight, lift legs up and down, pull down with right, lift up with left. Benefits are same as #3, but from a different angle.

5) **Bicycle**: In same position as face up leg lifts, pretend your riding a bicycle alternately bringing knees into chest then extending them rapidly. Breathe deep. Good cardiovascular exercise.

6) **Standing Leg Crosses**: Facing edge of pool, cross right leg over left extending it as far as possible. Then cross left leg over right in the same manner. Crossing the leg works the inner part of the thigh, extending it works the outer part.

7) **Leg Extensions**: Standing, hang onto the side of the pool for balance. Keeping leg straight, lift leg up as high as possible, then extend it back as far as possible. Do the same with the other leg. This works muscles in front and back of the thigh, buttocks muscles and hip flexors. Also good for the waist.

8) **Leg Circles**: Holding the edge of the pool with one hand, legs straight, make circles with each leg. Helps the muscles from the waist down.

9) **Dolphin Movement**: Holding the edge of the pool with both hands, bring both knees into the chest at the same time, then back out pushing water away from you. If not able, try alternating one leg at a time. Good for upper and lower abdomen.

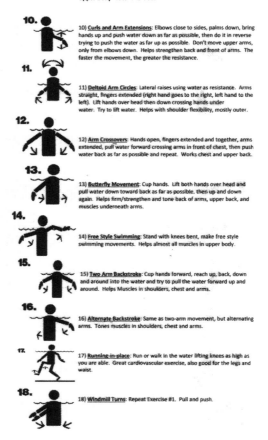

Upper Body Water Exercises:

10) **Curls and Arm Extensions**: Elbows close to sides, palms down, bring hands up and push water down as far as possible, then do it in reverse trying to push the water as far up as possible. Don't move upper arms, only from elbows down. Helps strengthen back and front of arms. The faster the movement, the greater the resistance.

11) **Deltoid Arm Circles**: Lateral raises using water as resistance. Arms straight, fingers extended (right hand goes to the right, left hand to the left). Lift hands over head then down crossing hands under water. Try to lift water. Helps with shoulder flexibility, mostly outer.

12) **Arm Crossovers**: Hands open, fingers extended and together, arms extended, pull water forward crossing arms in front of chest, then push water back as far as possible and repeat. Works chest and upper back.

13) **Butterfly Movement**: Cup hands. Lift both hands over head and pull water down toward back as far as possible, then up and down again. Helps firm/strengthen and tone back of arms, upper back, and muscles underneath arms.

14) **Free Style Swimming**: Stand with knees bent, make free style swimming movements. Helps almost all muscles in upper body.

15) **Two Arm Backstroke**: Cup hands forward, reach up, back, down and around into the water and try to pull the water forward up and around. Helps Muscles in shoulders, chest and arms.

16) **Alternate Backstroke**: Same as two-arm movement, but alternating arms. Tones muscles in shoulders, chest and arms.

17) **Running-in-place**: Run or walk in the water lifting knees as high as you are able. Great cardiovascular exercise, also good for the legs and waist.

18) **Windmill Turns**: Repeat Exercise #1. Pull and push.

Frank Sampedro I talked about Jack so much that my wife, Ipo, got tired of hearing it. She said that no one on the Big Island ever watched Jack or knew who he was! So, I asked a few random people at stores and they all knew who Jack was. She got a little more uppity and said I was only asking people from the mainland. So, when we were at Costco one day she said look, see that Hawaiian lady over there? I'm going to ask her. I saw the lady making faces at her. I was so surprised to hear what the lady told her, "Yes I know about Jack and I still do the face exercises!"

Frank "Crazy Horse" Sampedro
Rhythm guitarist for Neil Young

Face-A-Tonics

Because we are always fighting gravity, Jack included in his exercise program, exercises for the face. He would often tell his audience, "Don't let those 55 muscles in your face hang, droop, or sag. They all need to be worked just like the rest of the muscles in your body." He eventually came out with an exercise video just for the face called Face-A-Tonics.

LET'S FACE IT

Jack LaLanne's influence spans generations. As a publicist for assisted living and retirement communities, I often shared Jack's LaLanne-ism, videos and photographs with seniors to entertain and inspire them during their exercise sessions. But, I was always concerned about those residents not physically capable of fully participating in each facility's workouts. The solution came to me when Elaine (LaLa) sent Jack's "Face-A-Tonic" DVD.

It was the perfect solution for each person to participate in face exercises. Just about everyone recognized the handsome man in his trademark jump suit and very recognizable voice. "Look who it is!" — "I know him!" —"Remember him?" — "That's Jack LaLanne!" they'd say.

The seniors watched, listened to, and mimicked Jack's 20-minute routine as they lifted their eyebrows towards the tops of their heads. Jack spurred them on and encouraged them to "close your eyes as tight as you can. Open them wide. Move your mouth all the way to the left. Then, all the way to the right. Now blow your cheeks out. Hold it. Suck them back in." And, "Try to put your lips inside of your mouth. Lips in. Lips out."

As Jack kept prompting them, they would glance over to see each other's strange expressions including wide open mouths, frowns, fish-faces, chipmunk cheeks, squinted eyes, and especially grimaces.

Finishing up, Jack asked, "Doesn't that feel good? Now, inhale through your nose, hold it, exhale through your mouth. Isn't that relaxing? You're doing terrific!"

As the session ended, he sang his theme song with which he closed all of his TV shows and the seniors left with positive vibes as they once again worked out with Jack LaLanne.

Dee Dunheim
Publicist & feature story writer

The Magic Five

Upon waking at four in the morning, or sometimes even earlier, Jack would begin stretching and moving his face, neck and hands, then get up and do a few warm up exercises before going into the gym for an hour to do his workout with weights. He would then go into the pool and swim for an hour. If there was no pool, he would work out for two hours, wherever he happened to be. However, he did not expect everyone to do as he did; he was always testing himself.

This led to an idea for his lectures; to give away five exercises that attendees could take home with them. Hence, the birth of his MAGIC 5 EXERCISES. I can still hear him say in a lecture, "To get you started, you have to sit up to get out of bed, right? So, why not strengthen your stomach muscles with some crunches?" He would go through each exercise explaining their benefits. Known for his quick wit, he would say, very slowly, "AS YOU PASS OUT TODAY, (pause) be sure to pick up a copy of the MAGIC FIVE!"

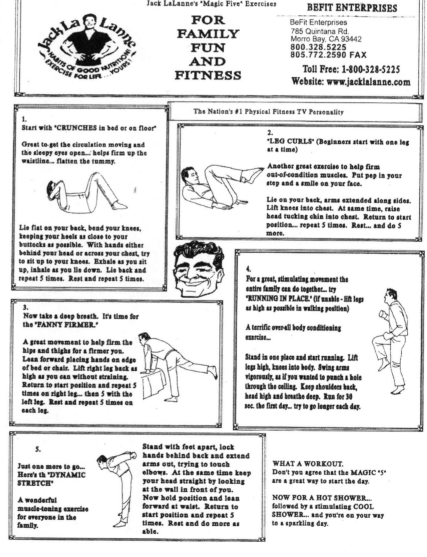

Jack LaLanne's "Magic Five" Exercises

BEFIT ENTERPRISES

FOR FAMILY FUN AND FITNESS

BeFit Enterprises
785 Quintana Rd.
Morro Bay, CA 93442
800.328.5225
805.772.2590 FAX

Toll Free: 1-800-328-5225
Website: www.jacklalanne.com

The Nation's #1 Physical Fitness TV Personality

1.
Start with "CRUNCHES in bed or on floor"

Great to get the circulation moving and the sleepy eyes open... helps firm up the waistline... flatten the tummy.

Lie flat on your back, bend your knees, keeping your heels as close to your buttocks as possible. With hands either behind your head or across your chest, try to sit up to your knees. Exhale as you sit up, inhale as you lie down. Lie back and repeat 5 times. Rest and repeat 5 times.

2.
"LEG CURLS" (Beginners start with one leg at a time)

Another great exercise to help firm out-of-condition muscles. Put pep in your step and a smile on your face.

Lie on your back, arms extended along sides. Lift knees into chest. At same time, raise head tucking chin into chest. Return to start position... repeat 5 times. Rest... and do 5 more.

3.
Now take a deep breath. It's time for the "FANNY FIRMER."

A great movement to help firm the hips and thighs for a firmer you. Lean forward placing hands on edge of bed or chair. Lift right leg back as high as you can without straining. Return to start position and repeat 5 times on right leg... then 5 with the left leg. Rest and repeat 5 times on each leg.

4.
For a great, stimulating movement the entire family can do together... try "RUNNING IN PLACE." (if unable - lift legs as high as possible in walking position)

A terrific over-all body conditioning exercise...

Stand in one place and start running. Lift legs high, knees into body. Swing arms vigorously, as if you wanted to punch a hole through the ceiling. Keep shoulders back, head high and breathe deep. Run for 30 sec. the first day... try to go longer each day.

5.
Just one more to go... Here's th 'DYNAMIC STRETCH'

A wonderful muscle-toning exercise for everyone in the family.

Stand with feet apart, lock hands behind back and extend arms out, trying to touch elbows. At the same time keep your head straight by looking at the wall in front of you. Now hold position and lean forward at waist. Return to start position and repeat 5 times. Rest and do more as able.

WHAT A WORKOUT.
Don't you agree that the MAGIC "5" are a great way to start the day.

NOW FOR A HOT SHOWER... followed by a stimulating COOL SHOWER... and you're on your way to a sparkling day.

Between the years of 1977 and 1983 on the national PBS show, *Over Easy*, with Hugh Downs, Jack periodically appeared as a guest, giving his expertise on exercise and nutrition. One time, Jack offered his "Magic Five" morning exercises. This resulted in a room full of requests! Guess who had to send them out? Your co-author, me!

Muscle Beach

Before I discovered Muscle Beach in Santa Monica, California, I would frequently go to Washington Park in Alameda, just outside Oakland, to work out on the rings, chinning, parallel and horizontal bars. It also had an expansive green grass area perfect for hand balancing, acrobatics, and tumbling. There I met Paul Knauer, a professional hand balancer and gymnastic coach from Germany. He noticed my raw unrefined talent and taught me the proper hand balancing and gymnastic techniques.

I had heard about Muscle Beach in Santa Monica where circus, gymnasts, and acrobatic performers honed and fine tuned their athletic prowess, along with teaching any one who was interested to try out their skills. I would often close my gym at 10 pm on a Friday night, leave one of my members in charge for the weekend, and drive 500 miles from Oakland to Santa

Monica, take a short nap, work out all day Saturday and Sunday, drive back and open my Physical Culture Studio at 5 am on Monday.

On one fateful day, I took a drive to muscle beach with my friend and student, Dr. Charlie McCarl. Upon arrival we noticed the guys were struggling with a trick. It was a three high on a backbend. My old wrestling buddy, Harold Zinkin, got the good fortune of being the guy on the bottom doing the backbend. When I asked everyone what was going on, they explained to me they have been working on this trick for two years. Apparently, the 3rd man up was the key component to hold that position. They were having a tough time finding someone who was up for the job. Guess who they delegated? 'Lil 'ol me! How was I to know I would be honored to be in this iconic photo? (Note, Charlie is the spotter, in the white trunks). Harold would inform me we were the

3 High on a Backbend—A legendary picture
Bottom, Harold Zinkin, DeForrest (Moe) Most, Jack (third man up), Gene Miller, on top.

first four men to perform this trick, and to his knowledge no one has ever duplicated it in the United States. That is one of the days I will never forget. This goes on my top 10 list. The sense of accomplishment was with me all the way home and for the rest of my life.

Jack LaLanne Health Spas – 30 Years Later

In the 1960's my television show was nationwide and even in some foreign countries. The show was shown in color across the United States and I was doing more and more personal appearances. During these appearances I had the opportunity to personally speak to thousands of students. Many of you expressed your love for the show but wanted even a more one-on-one experience in your daily exercise routine, a place to gather and share your experiences and even participate in group workouts or individual training. In the mid 1960's, we teamed up with a number of gym owners and came up with a working concept ultimately to be named, "The Jack LaLanne European Health Spas" in the west, and the "Jack LaLanne Health Spas" operated by Harry Schwartz in the eastern part of the United States. The plan was to open them in Los Angeles, New York, Miami, Chicago and many cities in between. We launched the first SPA in 1968 and thanks to you students, it was an overnight success. Elaine and I traveled extensively to help open and oversee each one of my new spas. It was heartwarming to see and talk with the members who expressed their enthusiasm and how they had improved their lives.

Lou Baratta I have always had such a high respect for Jack personally and in the industry of physical fitness. His participation in the Jack LaLanne European Health Spa was a successful time for us. Of course much of my time with Jack was business conversation, but I have some fond memories of our social time with him and Elaine. One thing that was impressive about Jack was when we were together socially, business conversation was avoided. One time we were having dinner in a local restaurant, Jack broke out in song. His voice was so good and he was so fun. I fondly remember Jack telling me that when he dies he will be teaching the angels about physical fitness! I'm sure the angels are more fit because of him.

Lou Baratta
Former execute of Jack LaLanne European Health Spas

Elaine: I have such high respect for the Baratta brothers: Joe, Carmen and Lou. They were instrumental in running the Jack LaLanne European Health Spas from the late 1960s to the end of the 1970s.

Dr. Robert M. Goldman When I was 11 or 12, I started training and watching Jack on TV. He was my initial inspiration to want to do the things he was able to do. As a teenager, I applied for a job at Jack LaLanne Health Clubs as a physical instructor and I was hired. At the time, there were no certified personal fitness trainers and no personal training certification programs. Richie Ornstein was my boss who trained and encouraged me because, out of admiration for Jack, I was trying to emulate some of the endurance records like hand-stand push-ups and chin-ups, some of which I finally accomplished, and eventually lead me to doing a spa commercial with him. When he came into the club for the shoot, he was a ball of fire, an unstoppable force with non-stop energy. It was like seeing your hero and mentor all in one shot. Later *Midday New York*, with Bill Boggs, wanted to do a show about Jack. Because of some of my endurance achievements, Richie sent me with Jack. We got to demonstrate strength and fitness exercises together and when asked, what got you started in fitness, in front of the world, I pointed my finger at Jack and said, "This is the guy right there, he was my inspiration and the reason for all my accomplishments."

Anyone who got to meet Jack knows that they were lucky to have interacted with him even for a moment. He was an inspiration for many to break world records including me.

Even as he got older, he was still an unstoppable force. Not many people could do different feats of strength every year for his birthday. I'm older now than when I first met him, and I'm trying to keep it going the same way, but Jack was one of a kind--a remarkable individual who was decades ahead of his time. He literally created and changed the entire fitness industry. He just did it.

Note: The following letter was written after Dr. Goldman met Jack at the WBBG Hall of Fame dinner. At the time, Dr. Goldman was working for Harry Schwartz and the Jack LaLanne Health Spas in New York and working on his medical degree. It involved an intensive independent study of androgenic anabolic steroids that he would later write a series of articles on the dangerous effects of anabolic steroids. Today he is known all over the world for his contributions to the medical community.

Rob Goldman
616 Beach 66 Street
Arverne, New York 11692

Dear Jack:

I hope you will remember me from the mass of fans that engulf you every-time you set foot in public. I wrote you last year about some gymnastic records. My dream came true when I was lucky enough to meet you in person at the WBBG hall of fame dinner honoring you. I was in awe of how fantastic you look in person. I don't think there is a bodybuilder around than can boast of a better V-shape.

I am winding up working for Mr. Schwartz and your spas here as I begin the next level of my medical education soon. I have been involved in an intensive independent study of androgenic anabolic steroids, and will be writing a series of articals on the dangerous effects in the #75 issue of Muscle Training Illustrated to be out in Feb. I will also be writing a number for medical journals as well as presently compiling a book for publication.

I hope you are enjoying the black and while lithographs I sent last year. Again, it was a remarkable experience meeting you in person. You were by far the most dynamic speaker, your presence and charisma was amazing. I clapped till my hands hurt. I was also fortunate enough to have a picture taken with you of which I had a blow up made. You probably hang on the wall in more peoples homes than Farrah Faucett Majors.

Thank you again Jack for the inspiration you have provided me to redo my old records. The only disappoitment from the luncheon is that I would have really liked to hear you sing. Well, maybe next time.

All the best,

bob goldman

Dr. Robert M. Goldman, **MD, PhD, DO, FAASP**

World Chairman-International Medical Commission, Co-Founder & Chairman of the Board-A4M, Founder & Chairman-International Sports Hall of Fame, Co-Founder & Chairman-World Academy of Anti-Aging Medicine, President Emeritus-National Academy of Sports Medicine (NASM), Chairman-U.S. Sports Academy's Board of Visitors

SECTION FOUR

Nutrition

"The food you eat today is walking and talking and you are wearing it tomorrow."
– LaLanne-ism

You Are An Architect

I like to think that we can all be architects of our bodies because our bodies are much like the houses we live in. Our body houses our minds, souls, bones, muscles and internal organs; all of which allow the body to function.

If you have a man-made house and if it isn't cared for over the years, it deteriorates, becomes non-functional. The plumbing breaks down, the foundation starts to collapse, the central heating system goes haywire, and the exterior has to be done over. In other words that house is a wreck and it looks old and dilapidated.

It is the same with the human house. If neglected, the foundation--206 bones and 648 muscles--may start to collapse. The internal plumbing won't work regularly and the central heating system, your body's ability to stand hot and cold, may not operate properly. The exterior of your human house becomes old and tired looking. The texture of your skin loses its youthful appearance. Your hair and eyes lose their luster. The message is clear, if you don't care for your human house it also goes to pot and deteriorates.

Now let's focus on what can be done to rebuild your human house. If you were going to rebuild your man made house you would first draw up a plan. Do the same with your human house. Start with a plan.

1. Plan to eat a sensible diet including more fresh fruits and vegetables to keep the internal plumbing system (bowels, bladder, arteries, veins, etc.) working properly. Leading health authorities recommend that you eat at least five servings of fruits and vegetables every day, along with a variety of other foods. Include those fruits and vegetables that are high in vitamins A & C. Also, are you getting enough fiber in your diet?

2. Plan to get enough vitamins and minerals to keep the electrical and heating system in shape. I use a complete multi-vitamin plus the antioxidant vitamins (the best known are B, C, and beta carotene) that help fight cancer and heart disease.

3. Now the external structure of your human house, the muscles and the bones.

    a. Make a plan for a systematic exercise program. You need both strength and aerobic work. 30 minutes a day, three or four times a week, should be enough in the beginning and you can increase the intensity as you progress.

    b. To build up your bones you'll need calcium, magnesium, and vitamin D along with your exercise program.

    c. When you are getting ample nutrients and sufficient exercise your skin will be more youthful. Your eyes, the windows of your soul, will be more alert, your hair more radiant, and your nails stronger.

In theory, we have completely rebuilt your body from the inside out. Who will get the credit? You will! So become that building contractor and architect for your human house.

"Eat foods in their natural state as much as possible." – *Jack LaLanne*

Eat Right And You Can't Go Wrong!

Healthy! Lean! Full of energy! Youthful! Every human being wants to feel this way. This desire for wholeness is something we all share. But at the same time it's something that seems to elude us all.

Jack's approach to nutrition takes us back to grass-roots, when life and food were simple. Agriculture and food processing has taken some of the whole, natural nutrition out of the food we eat.

Have we lost touch with our taste and desire for real food? Modern day food processing and farming has broadened our menu choices, but has it boosted our health?

As omnivores, we are faced with the widest possible range of food choices. We eat both plants and animals, but do we have the right balance? While protein in the diet is important, the reality is, we probably eat too much animal protein. Scientist and nutritional author, Michael Pollen, put it succinctly and elegantly in his book, *The Eaters Manifesto,* which touts that we should, "Eat food, not too much, mostly plants." Could he be onto something?

Jack LaLanne said it in a similar way years ago when he declared, EAT RIGHT AND YOU CAN'T GO WRONG. "It's not what you do some of the time that counts, it's what you do most of the time that counts. If you do everything in moderation you can't go wrong."

In one of his writings he observes the health of the nation. "As you look over America, how many healthy people do you know? How many happy people do you know? There are millions and millions of Americans today that neglect themselves so much that they're not getting any fun out of life. As I've said many times in my lectures and seminars, Americans often die at 60 but they're buried at 75 or 80. They've missed out on so much of their life."

Tomorrow Is What You Eat Today (Excerpt From *Live Young Forever,* 2009)

I believe most foods that have been tampered with or manufactured by man, or even foods that have undergone an attempt at improvement, are less than perfect and are, in all likelihood, bad for our long-term health. What am I talking about? I'm talking about food coloring, preservatives, thickeners, thinners, so-called taste enhancers and the zillion other chemicals thrown into the foods we are buying and ingesting every day, week after week, year after year. In addition, we are also eating meat, fish and poultry and produce that has been treated or dosed up with a variety of hormones, antibiotics and chemicals. It doesn't take a genius to realize if we eat products that have been loaded up with poor-quality or even distinctly harmful ingredients then those same ingredients will be passed down to our own bodies.

In many ways we are lucky today. There is an abundance of farmer's markets, grocery and specialty stores that can deliver fine health-giving produce. But we simply have to shop intelligently. Make it a rule to always buy the freshest, most nourishing of mineral-rich foods.

You've heard it a thousand times: You are what you eat. What you eat today will be walking and talking tomorrow. Food is what we use to build and repair our body tissue. The quality of your blood, brain and muscles will be in direct relation to the quality of the food you eat.

Think clearly before you enter your local grocery store. Determine before you enter that you will buy only foods that will contribute to your health and that of your family. And while you're at it, look down the street from your supermarket. See the offices of doctors, dentists, druggists and medical clinics? Their bills run into thousands of dollars, and a large proportion of their customers are there not only because they have ignored the basic health principles of controlling alcohol and tobacco, but because they have chosen, through ignorance or indifference, to eat junk foods.

The River Of Life- Your Bloodstream

As Americans attempt to save the environment, most of them still pollute and poison their own bodies – those personal and precious environments over which they have complete clean-up control.

For example, "a river, with its tributary creeks, brooks and streams, is like the human bloodstream, with its thousands of miles of arteries, veins and capillaries."

When garbage and refuse enter a stagnant body of water, poisons and impurities accumulate. Without rapid water movement, they get stuck and pollute the river. Likewise, when we eat meat, dairy products, sugars, salts and fats, the wastes slowly decompose in our intestines and accumulate in our tissues. Without exercise, our blood stream can't flow properly to flush out the poisons.

It is well known that athletes can eat just about anything and get away with it. That's because they metabolize food quickly – even if it's junk! High levels of activity allow their bodies to quickly rid themselves of impurities through natural elimination. They burn up poisons! Exhale them! Sweat them out! Now just think how healthy an athletic person can be when he or she also eats nutritious foods.

Imagine regular exercise and nutritious food as 'nature's broom' gently sweeping out your intestinal tract. Cleanliness of the bowels results in proper elimination, quickly manifesting itself in all the cells of your body. You'll feel more dynamic, notice improved skin tone, shinier hair, brighter eyes; fresher breath and even a revitalized sex drive!

When I first started preaching nutrition and diet reform, they called me a wavy-haired fitness nut, a crackpot, a laughing stock, but I've been saying it, *and proving it*, for years: "If man makes it, don't eat it!"

Gale Shemwell Rudolph, PhD I met Jack and Elaine when finishing up my PhD in Nutrition at UCLA, near their Hollywood home. He was looking for someone to help with a cookbook he wanted to write.

Often while having dinner at the LaLanne home, Jack would remind us that our bloodstream was our ' River of Life." He probed the latest nutrition research, often asking questions about "instant breakfast" concepts as he had developed the first one which was soy-protein-based. At one dinner, Hattie, their housekeeper, made some fried chicken. Jack removed all the crispy skin. Elaine reached over and took a bite. Jack never criticized this; he never chastised someone for smoking or being fat. He only encouraged people to be better and preached that it is what you do most of the time that counts.

In those yearsJack met many of my UCLA and Carnation Company friends. He was so welcoming. He'd engage them in their interests, once encouraging a friend to keep up wrestling and explaining how good wrestling was for fitness. Basically, anything that got you moving was endorsed; it didn't have to be his own regimens.

He had a great sense of humour, too and when someone would say to him, "I used to watch you with my mother," he'd quip "I spent a lot of time on the floor with your mother!"

Gale Shemwell Rudolph, **PhD**
Certified Nutrition Specialist and Certified Food Scientist.

"Variety! Variety! Variety! If you eat carrots for the rest of your life, you'd be bored." – LaLanne-ism

Jack's Ideas on Diet

(Excerpt from original 1969 Fawcett Publication, *Jack LaLanne's Diet and Exercise Guide*. Also reference "Cooking with Jack" (2005), a collection of recipes and nutritional guidelines.)

Since I was 15, my philosophy has been based on my experience as a nutrition pioneer. It has involved intensive study and experimentation, with just about every diet you can think of and can be summed up in one sentence: Correct eating does not mean staying on a boring, rigid diet that never varies. It is a matter of not overindulging. Just eat good, wholesome foods in their natural state as much as possible. It's really as simple as that.

What do I mean by food in its natural state? I mean fresh, wholesome food that has been prepared to maintain its full nutritional value as much as Mother Nature intended. Therefore, to me, proper preparation of food is essential because food is the "clay" we use to build and repair body tissues. As I have said many times before, I believe our lives are based on three ingredients: **exercise, what we eat, and what we believe**. If we keep stuffing the wrong kind of food down our stomachs, we're eventually going to pay the price.

What would happen if you put water in your gas tank? Your car wouldn't run, would it? Well, what do you think happens when you put inferior "fuel" into your body? You eventually wouldn't run too well, either! Many people wonder why they are worn out and listless all of the time. They may have run out of gas, that's why.

This isn't too surprising, actually. In fact, I have felt for many years that we Americans are the most over-fed, undernourished nation in the world. This is pretty hard to believe when you take into consideration the quality and quantity of crops that are available every year to each one of us.

According to a recent report I read from the United States Department of Agriculture, twenty percent of America's population eats nutritionally poor diets. The report also stated that this decline of the American diet is the first recorded since the Department started taking surveys back in 1936.

It has nothing to do with whether you're rich or poor, it simply means the American public must have more knowledge about what to eat and then have the willpower to follow a good, well-balanced nutritional eating program. In order to do this, we must include in our diet foods from the basic food groups of grains, vegetables, fruits, dairy, meat and beans.

I have been preaching the philosophy of balance between food intake and physical activity demonstrating that exercise is a most important component to leading a healthy lifestyle for over 70 years. I know many of you have heard me say, "*Exercise is king, nutrition is queen, put them together and you have a kingdom. What I eat today, I am wearing tomorrow. If I put inferior foods in my body today, I'm going to be inferior tomorrow. It's that simple. The size of your slacks depends on the size of your snacks.*"

John Westerdahl When I was a college student at Loma Linda University, Jack was a great inspiration to me as I pursued the health sciences and the field of nutrition as a career. His TV show, his lectures, and books, emphasized the importance of a diet rich in vegetables, fruits, whole grains, and lean protein. He stressed the value of juicing. He developed many state of the art nutritional products that contributed to advancing health education and practical knowledge of nutrition to the public. He was my hero and role model, and I am honored to have known him personally and as a friend for 40 years. One of the highlights of my life was to be an invited guest to exercise with Jack on his TV show.

He would never come out with or endorse a product unless it included exercise and nutrition together. Combining exercise and nutrition is a large component of his legacy.

John Westerdahl, PhD, MPH, RDN, FAND
Registered Dietitian Nutritionist and Health Scientist

One of the most important aspects of a physical fitness program is good nutrition. Fad diets come and go, and often return again. But the basis for physical fitness remains constant: eat right so you can't go wrong. You wouldn't wake up your dog in the morning and give him a cup of coffee, a cigarette, and a donut. That would kill the dog!

Our bodies are remarkable. Our cells have the ability to regenerate frequently so it makes sense that what you put in your mouth today will show itself later. It's like planting a garden. What you sow today, you'll reap tomorrow.

What does the word "diet" mean to you? Is it what you eat every day? Or does it mean hunger, calories, a temporary state, or regimented eating? The first thought that comes into my mind when I hear the word "diet" is temporary. Most people who go on a diet end up going off and on and off and on. They lose weight, gain weight, lose weight, and gain weight. It's a vicious cycle that accomplishes little and isn't particularly healthy either.

The Dieter Profile

Can you identify with any of these various types of "dieters"? Note: If you take in more calories than you burn up, you won't won't lose weight. It's that simple.

- The **Picker, Taster, or Snacker**. Glorial couldn't understand why she gained weight. "Oh, I hardly eat anything all day, and I still gain," she complained. Then one day, her niece came to visit and pointed out how many times Gloria grabbed a"quick" snack during the day. The Picker picks all day, and each pick has calories. The Glorias of the world are like the newspaper business. Years ago newspapers sold for only two cents each, but that created empires. The Picker also starts small, but builds a big corporation (usually in front) before he or she realizes it.

- The **One-Mealer**. Alan ate just one meal a day in the evening, and still gained weight. Findings show that many people who do not eat all day long overeat at the evening meal, and without realizing it, take in more calories than if they had eaten three regular meals. They don't burn up all those calories and the spread takes over.

- The **Hidden-Calories Dieter**. Alissa has good intentions. She drinks coffee wth no cream, but loads it with sugar; eats a cottage cheese salad for lunch, but tops it off with pie a la mode; broils a lean steak, but stuffs the 75-calorie baked potato with butter and sour cream. You get the picture.

- The **Over-Indulger**. George carefully selects only healthy foods, yet he always eats too much at one sitting. One apple a day is good, so why eat 10 of them?

It Isn't What You Do

It isn't what you *do*, it's what you *don't do*. This applies to most facets of our lives. What do I mean? For example, if you have one thousand dollars in the bank and you spend two thousand then you are bankrupt.

Maybe you are saying to yourself, "Jack, what does this have to do with our health and physical condition in general?"

1. If you eat 6000 calories a day and don't exercise then you are going to be a real fatty. If you exercise regularly and vigorously then you can handle the 6000 calories.

   Take the example of champion athletes. Football players, swimmers, basketball players, etc., eat maybe 6 to 10 thousand calories a day. But they exercise so long and hard that they burn up the calories. As I've said so many times, we are combustion engines just like our cars. The faster you drive your car, the more fuel it consumes.

If you drive your car 100 miles an hour, it will burn double the fuel. The slower you drive the less fuel you will burn. Just like your body, the more you exercise, the more fuel or calories you burn. So you see, it isn't what you *do*, it's what you *don't do*.

2. If you drink alcohol or consume too much sugar you are destroying B-complex vitamins. There are about 12 to 15 different B vitamins of which 6 are absolutely essential.

3. If you use any kind of caffeine (coffee, tea, soft drinks, etc.) you destroy a very important antioxidant, vitamin E. They did many, many tests on truck drivers who drink excessive amounts of caffeine and found that most of them had a vitamin E deficiency.

4. If you smoke you will destroy another essential vitamin, vitamin C.

5. If you don't eat enough roughage or fiber you will have faulty elimination.

6. If you lift weights and don't get enough aerobic work you are out of balance, but if you add 12 to 15 minutes of aerobics three to four times a week, you are right on target.

7. I believe in a daily vitamin supplement. Most foods today are picked green, over-processed, stored, and over-cooked. Most fruits and vegetables are subjected to artificial fertilizers, insecticides and pesticides. All of this can destroy valuable vitamins, minerals and enzymes. So, I feel it is a must to supplement your diet daily with extra vitamins and minerals. And again I'll state, *it isn't what you do, it's what you don't do.*

If one apple is good, a hundred isn't." – LaLanne-ism

Your Waistline Is Your Lifeline

FAT equates to Fatal—Alarming—Trouble. The human body needs fat, but the stuff should be in our bodies not ON them. It seems that a great majority of people want to lose weight but there are so many diets and plans available that the choice is bewildering. Going on a "crash diet" you can indeed lose weight but if you don't exercise you end up with a bunch of flab, all in the wrong places. Without muscle tone the flesh just hangs and sags.

It seems that everything to do with losing weight is predicated on the scale. I believe that its importance is highly exaggerated. Why? Because the scale doesn't tell you about what kind of improvement you have made to your body. That's why I advocate checking with your tape measure. Most people want good proportions, the ratio of chest to waist to hips. This is as important to men as it is to women. We all can't be taller or shorter, nor can we be Mr./Ms. or Mrs. America. The key is that everyone can be well proportioned. The whole secret of making the most of yourself, is taking what you have and putting it where you want it and the best place to start is your waistline.

I hear this story all the time, "Jack, I weigh the same as I did in high school." Then I ask, "Is your waistline the same size?" "Well, no, it's three or four inches larger, but I weigh the same." There is the key. This person has lost muscle tone and replaced it with killer fat, so I believe the best place to begin to re-proportion your body is your waistline. Besides benefiting your good looks, keeping your waist trim is important for health reasons. The less fat you have to carry around, the more energy you acquire. Every pound of excess weight puts a needless strain on the heart. The scale measures your weight and the tape measure is a tool to help you accomplish your goal of perfect measurements.

The Battle Of The Bulge

(Chapter 17 Revitalize Your life, 2003)

People often kid themselves when they look in the mirror because they see themselves from the neck up. Use a full-length mirror for constructive criticism. Stand nude before your mirror. Don't hold in your breath. Don't tighten your stomach muscles, buttocks, or biceps. Turn around slowly and examine yourself full-face, profile left, profile right, and rear view. Be honest, what do you see? If you see skin that is starting to hang and sag, a double chin, inches of loose flesh at your waist and underarms, it's time to tell yourself, "the sands of time shifted" and do something about it!

Unfortunately, without a fitness program, Americans seem quite susceptible to bulges. "Middle-age spread," "the corporation," "cellulite." I use these terms to bring home the fact that we must fight against this problem with exercise and proper nutrition.

Fat accumulates on parts of the body where there's least activity. When there is no activity, fat likes to hibernate and find a place where it can go to sleep. That's where its friends, the other fats, gather to hang, sag, and droop. Fat is also like a river, it will flow to whatever part of the body that has the least resistance.

Richie Ornstein I was working as an instructor at the Jack LaLanne Spa in Manhattan, New York after leaving the New York Police Department. A man came in and asked, "Hey, buddy. Will you hold me down?" He went to the lat machine, and he pulled down the entire rack of plates while I held him down. Then he turned around and said, "Will you hand me those dumbbells." I said, "You're Jack LaLanne." "Right," he said. "Now, let's go." From that time on, we became good friends.

I learned about Jack on TV from my younger 5 year old brother who followed Jack's teaching and became a pro wrestler, "Wildman Jack Armstrong."

Jack also helped to create the Mister and Miss New York's Finest Bodybuilding Championship contest for the New York Police Department to show that cops don't always eat donuts, bagels and coffee. To inspire the cops to get fit, Jack created a program called, "U Auto Exercise" for the times when they were parked.

Jack was just Jack! One day, I took him to my gym in Greenwich Village were I worked out. When Jack walked in, the owner said, "I thought I saw God." Everyone went wild as Jack enthusiastically answered all of their questions.

Richie Ornstein
Producer, The Joe Franklin National TV Show, NYC Police Detective, Personal Trainer

---

My friend Richie Ornstein, a retired New York detective, was in just such a state. He cleaned his plate at every meal, stuffed himself with junk food between meals, and was 50 pounds overweight. He went on diet after diet but could never stay on them because he was always hungry. I explained to him that he could actually eat off his weight by eating three meals a day or even five meals a day if he would only put the proper fuel in his mouth and exercise regularly. I told him that anything in life is possible but he had to make it happen and to set a goal for himself and go for it.

He wrote this note to me:

I lost 50 pounds and over 10 inches from my waistline. I learned that there was no such word as impossible in the LaLanne dictionary if you believe in yourself and set reasonable long- and short-term goals. Here are some of my do's and don'ts I learned from you Jack:

- Don't eat until you are stuffed. Practice leaving some food on the plate.
- Don't give in to temptation when you go to parties. Use common sense and substitute junk food with salads and healthy food.
- Don't reward yourself with junk food because you have lost some weight or inches. Reward yourself with clothes or something you can't eat.
- Eat foods in their natural state with as much variety as you can.
- Modify your lifestyle to fit your new way of taking care of yourself. You didn't put on the extra pounds overnight, so don't expect them to go away instantly. Be patient and you will reach your goals.

As I emphasized to Richie, if you want to get your waist down you must eat and exercise it off. Your waist is four sided--the front, two sides and the back, and all sides need exercise.

The more you exercise the faster you are going to burn up the calories. Also, when you are burning these extra calories it is important to keep your daily caloric intake to about 1500 calories or less. Strive to get your waistline down to what it was in your prime.

Anything cardiovascular, fifteen to twenty minutes or more three or four times a week, such as walking, running, swimming, bicycling, and even working out with weights (if you don't rest between sets) burns up fat. The harder you breathe, the more oxygen you take into your bloodstream and the faster you burn up fat. It's very similar to your fireplace: The more air you give your fire the faster it burns. I like to think of us as combustion engines, the more we eat and the less we exercise the slower the fat burns, but the less we eat and the more we exercise the faster we burn and lose the fat. The body is a wonderful thing the harder it works the stronger it becomes.

A note from Dr. Robert Goldman: It is rare to have a mentor, friend and brother in the health field equal to Richie Ornstein, fondly known as 'Richie O'. I met him while working at the Jack LaLanne Health Clubs in New York as a teenager. One could never ask for a more giving, kind, caring, modest, generous and easy going boss and all around superstar embodying the Jack LaLanne creed; a friendship journey that lasted over 45 years. Richie passed away late 2021. He will always be remembered and respected.

Dining Out With Jack

Elaine Jack was often recognized in restaurants, and people would love to come over to our table and want to talk to him. He would stop and greet them even if he had a fork in his hand ready to put into his mouth. He never said no to anyone who wanted a picture, an autograph or an answer to a question. If someone was having a birthday or special celebration, he would often go over to their table and sing Happy Birthday or if it was a woman, he'd sing, "If You Were The Only Girl In The World."

Jack was a singer? Yes, many people did not know he had a beautiful singing voice.

Despite Jack taking time for his meet and greets and serenading at restaurants, he remained steadfast and meticulous about his eating habits, as he explains below.

Remember as I have always said, it's not what you do some of the time, it's what you do most of the time that counts. So if you are dining at a restaurant and you are counting your calories it is only a problem if you allow it to be so. In 80 percent of food-providing establishments, you will be able to find acceptable nourishment that will not contribute to fat and calorie accumulation.

With a warm smile, explain with gentleness that you eat a special diet. You might ask for fresh vegetables, a baked potato, without butter or sour cream, and your fish without sauce. When you have soup, ask if it's broth based as opposed to cream based. Personally, I love soup. I always ask for a special salad of 8 to 10 raw vegetables, with no dressing. You can ask for Balsamic vinegar and olive oil on the side. Want a dessert? How about berries or a fresh fruit salad?

Having breakfast out? You can go for hot oatmeal (no sugar-loaded cereals), with fresh berries or some honey if you want a sweetener. Try a vegetarian egg-white omelet and ask that it be cooked in a little vegetable or olive oil, not butter. A slice of whole-grain toast without butter is readily available. Most restaurants have yogurt. I love it with prunes. Personally I don't drink tea or coffee, but a cup or two a day isn't sinfully bad, preferably without cream and sugar. Elaine prefers to choose from the large variety of herbal teas available.

Dining out can easily sabotage your fitness goals. Because Elaine and I dined out frequently, we learned years ago to enjoy the experience and we always maintained control of what we consumed. Many restaurant eaters make the mistakes of loading up on bread before the meal even begins. Worse, they add butter. Then they have two or three cocktails and nibble on other goodies. They overeat at the beginning and then are satiated prior to the main course and hardly enjoy the outing. If you really want an appetizer, ask for some raw veggies without the dip.

Before you go into a restaurant, I want you to stop at the entrance and make a promise to yourself not to weaken when you see the menu or hear the waiter talk about the restaurant specials.

A frequent occurrence at restaurants is the failure of the chef to listen to the waiter's request. Salads have a fat- and calorie-dense dressing poured over them. The egg-white omelet has cheese in it (most cheese is more than 50 percent fat, by calories). A dollop of cream has been arranged prettily in the middle of your soup bowl. The whole-grain toast has butter on it. Your baked potato is covered in sour cream. So what do you do? I'll tell you what 80 percent of diners do. They accept it and chow down! What you should do is pick up the plate and hand it back to the waiter, reminding him of what you actually ordered.

Dining Out In San Francisco

Note from Elaine: My second date with Jack was lunch at a Japanese restaurant in San Francisco. As we entered I noticed he had a bag in his hand. The owner and staff greeted him as he handed one of them the bag. I was curious but being our second date I didn't ask. When lunch was served it came with rice, brown rice. He told me he brings his brown rice to the restaurant because they don't get enough requests for brown rice. In fact none. People were used to white rice. This was in the 1950's. Salads on the side with dinner consisted mostly of lettuce, greens and maybe a little tomato. I remember one night when Jack asked for a salad with raw vegetables and mushrooms. I can still hear the appalled waiter saying "RAW MUSHROOMS!?" Jack's studio was in Oakland and on Tuesday, Thursday, and Saturday he would often go out to dinner with his friends in San Francisco, and he would often meet me at 6 o'clock when I got off the air from the 90-minute daily TV show.

John's Grill is one of the restaurants that is still there. Back in the 1950's Gus, the owner, loved Jack and his sense of humor and his philosophy of life. He even named a salad after him. His son, John, who now runs the restaurant, organized a Jack LaLanne day for Jack's 90th birthday, complete with a vintage fire engine that drove Jack all over his haunts in San Francisco. The Jack LaLanne Salad is still on the menu.

North Beach Restaurant was also a place we loved to go and it is still there and famous for its Tuscan food. Lorenzo and Bruno were always there to greet us with friendship and a welcoming smile.

Original Joe's on Taylor street, a short distance from the KGO-TV studios at the time, is where we spent many a night after I got off the air and often sat at the counter and enjoyed many good Italian American dishes. After a fire they moved to North Beach and also have a restaurant in San Jose. Both restaurants are still putting out the same quality food.

Because of his eating habits, Jack was never demanding and all the restaurants respected that.

Dining Out In Los Angeles

Musso & Frank Grill When we moved to Los Angeles in 1959 we found a number of restaurants we loved, however, many are no longer there. One restaurant that has stood the test of time and was reminiscent of our life in San Francisco was, and still is, Musso & Franks Grill. Having opened in 1919, it is the oldest, and one of the most famous restaurants in Hollywood. On September 27, 2019 they celebrated 100 years serving the public and Hollywood legends.

Wolfgang Puck We lived in the Hollywood Hills from 1959 to 1986 and also found good restaurants. It was 1975 when we heard about this great new restaurant called Ma Maison so we headed over to taste the cuisine. There we met Wolfgang Puck. Not only did he have great food but a great personality. In fact, it was magnetic. You couldn't help but like him but he also liked his customers. He became so popular he opened Spago Restaurant on the Sunset Strip in Beverly Hills and further launched many companies. He catered a pre-celebration party the night before Jack received his star on the Hollywood Walk of Fame.

Both Jack and Wolfgang loved to quip. I don't know who had more quips, Wolfgang or Jack, but they both made you laugh. While at HSN, during a 24-hour period, we would do eight to ten-minute live segments promoting the Jack LaLanne Power Juicer. Often we would be back to back with Wolfgang Puck who would come on either before or after us. Frequently Jack would go on Wolfgang's set and admire his knives, pots and pans and then Wolfgang would come on our set and taste the juice. One day Wolfgang came on our set and tasted the juice and said, "Mmmmmm. This would go good with Vodka!" Needless to say Wolfgang and Jack received a memo from "the Tower" that neither one of them would be able to come on each other's set again.

Dimitris Houndalas, Le Petit Greek Restaurant Jack was an inspiration to me in so many ways. He had a fierce dedication to fitness. He was groundbreaking in bringing fitness and health to the everyday household. He constantly explored what that body and mind was capable of. He created his own menu at the restaurant and ate as disciplined as he worked out. I am the same way and I know it drives my family crazy on vacation, but I like that I am not alone in this zealousness to my health.

When I first met him, he asked me to punch him in the stomach. I was in my late twenties and in excellent shape. He had to be in his 70's. I didn't want to hurt him and so I cautiously punched him, and he yelled "harder" and he pushed me until I really punched him. You have to imagine we are in the restaurant in a packed dining room. His abs were like rocks! He was so strong and so sure of himself. He had charisma and charm and was always gracious to those who wanted to say hello. He knew how to work the crowd.

He would joke with me, "Are you a Greek God or a goddamn Greek?" We always laughed as I replied, "A little of both." I asked him one time, "What is the secret?" and he said, "You have to find a routine and stick to it every day for the rest of your life." He would also say, "I hate working out, but I love the results." Now I don't know if I really believed that. He had a passion for working out, but I do believe he was tapping into the resistance most people feel when they exercise which is why he emphasized the results are more important than whether you like the process or not. He was right, the results are well worth it; health, strength, flexibility, endurance, agility. Physical strength and discipline were created by a mental discipline and commitment which can then be applied to many aspects of life.

He had told me you have to see working out like a bank account. You put something in every day to build it up. That resonated with me.

But the thing he said that I keep thinking about now is, "It is what it is, Dimitris." He refused to allow himself to get riled up. He had a certain amount of acceptance of that which cannot be changed; not that peaceful buddha like acceptance, but a type of acceptance coupled with determination and inner strength.

For a fitness and health fanatic like myself, from Nafplio, Greece, meeting Jack was a dream come true. It was an honor and privilege to know him. The older I get the more inspirational his memory is to me. His commitment to health & fitness is bar none and most importantly it never altered with age.

Dimitris Houndalas
Proprietor & General Manager,
Le Petit Greek Estiatorio, in Los Angeles.

"Energy makes people beautiful. That's what charisma is." – LaLanne-ism

Dining Out In New York

Sal Scognamillo Patsy's New York For over 50 years every time Jack LaLanne was in New York he came into our restaurant, either with Elaine, family or alone.

I always remember him being so vital, happy, and loyal to us. One of his sayings was "Patsy's food fills you up, not out." Whenever he came in, all the customers would recognize him, want to speak with him and relate stories of the positive influence he had in their lives. He would be so generous with his time telling stories, taking photos, and just talking with all the customers. He had great discipline and never deviated from his eating habits. I think his favorite meal was grilled salmon. I also fondly remember how he would take time, when asked, to even give advice and demonstrate some of his exercises to the customers. It gave them great joy.

Another great memory is when celebrity customers like Frank Sinatra, Tony Bennett, Danny Aleillo and Tony Danza would share their stories about the influence Jack had on their lives. He was a great man. I was so honored to know him!

Sal Scognamicco
Patsy's Restaurant, New York

Tony Danza I'm old enough to remember being in our living room in Brooklyn and watching my mother and my aunt Francis as they exercised along with Jack. As they put it, "It's the great Jack LaLanne on TV!" They'd be standing holding the back of a chair, lifting their legs behind them in unison with Jack in his unitard. Only he could get away with wearing that outfit as I found out years later, when he was a guest on my talk show. To welcome him I wore one of his unitards. On him, it looked good, on me it didn't. But I did get in it!

Whenever and wherever I saw Jack, whether on the set or at some fancy gala, I would always feel so great when he would go out of his way to say hello to me. That usually consisted of a little stand up wrestling and I could feel his strength as he laughed and asked if I had been keeping in shape. I always felt special that Jack LaLanne knew me.

Getty Images taken in New York at Jack's 90th birthday party.

But he wasn't only a friend, he was a huge inspiration. As I've gotten older my appreciation and amazement at how easy he made growing older look, has only grown. Someone once said about getting old, that it's tough to do it with dignity. Jack LaLanne did it with such dignity.

It's hard to compute how important Jack's contribution is to the health and well-being of people all over the world, but, for my mom, my aunt, and me, it was huge! I am so proud to have known the great Jack LaLanne, and even more proud that he knew me.

Tony Danza
Actor, television personality

Dining Out In Morro Bay

I would be remiss if I didn't mention the restaurants in Morro Bay that we frequented and tolerated Jack and I as we dined out.

The restaurants we haunted in the seaside town of Morro Bay were mostly Dorn's, The Galley, China Dragon, Bayside Café, Great American Fish Company, The Harbor Hut, and others that are no longer there. Jack never shunned anyone. When approached by someone who recognized him he would answer their questions, give them an autograph and as mentioned even sing for them. There were many renditions of 'Happy Birthday' and "If You Were the Only Girl in the World" sung by Jack to customers.

The Harbor Hut at one time had a paddle wheel boat called the Tiger's Folly on which we had many birthday parties as it cruised around the bay for two hours, with our friends. We would never have a dinner party on the boat without resident musician, and owner of Goofy Graphics, Gary Ryan. As Gary recollects, "The best part of the cruise was the 'Talent Show' after dinner. Everybody, including Jack, Elaine and the famous got up and did something. It was absolutely the best show in town and totally unrehearsed. At the spur-of-the-moment, guests would ask, 'Do you know this tune?' I never knew what tunes or keys they might ask for, but I accompanied them all and several asked me if I would like to go on the road with them. The perfect dinner cruise ender."

Jack often visited Gary's business, Goofy Graphics while he was in town. Here's what it was like to have Jack pop in.

"Jack's here," a heads-up call from my shop employees.

Sure enough, a close-by parking spot was open and Jack swooped in, corvette and all. His entrance was always upbeat, smiling, happy and full of energy. He'd hug my daughter, high-five the staff, regardless of who was in the shop at the time. Then the fun started. Customers would wonder what was going on, why did everyone light up when this guy popped in?

Invariably, the light would go on for the customer, and the reaction was always the same, and we'd wait for it…

"You're…you're…you're HIM!"

The staff would crack up, as it happened every time. It was him!

By the time Jack was ready to move on, he had the customers and staff doing squats, lifts and other creative moves, and walked out to applause.

Dining In. Hints from Jack

Now let's go out to a dinner party where the hosts pride themselves on the elegance of their cuisine. Whereas no one can force you to eat something you don't want, you will have to exercise a little caution in your approach. A good host won't insist you eat food when you decline politely. The problem is being too unbending or forceful in your refusal which can make the host uncomfortable and even give the other guests the feeling they are doing something wrong. If you feel you can't mention you are being careful in your diet, pass on something you don't want and eat more of what you do want. Or simply take very small portions. Avoid the gravies and dressings on the table. Remove the skin from the fish or chicken. Should your host insist you try her favorite dessert, take the smallest portion and let most of it remain on your plate. Above all, be polite and use some discipline.

Maria Shriver What always impressed me about Jack was his zest for life, his discipline, his passion, his enthusiasm and of course his love for you (Elaine). I remember sitting with you both at the Arnold classic many years ago and you were having dinner. I sat down with you both and he talked about the importance of good nutrition and discipline and what to eat and what not to eat.

Maria Shriver
American journalist, author and founder of non-profit organization,
The Women's Alzheimer's Movement

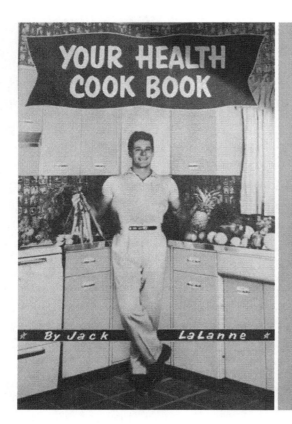

YOUR HEALTH COOK BOOK

By Jack LaLanne

PREFACE

by JACK LA LANNE

You Are What You Eat

Are you satisfied with your present physical condition?

Do you measure up to the splendid specimen of beautiful womanhood, or superb manhood that you SHOULD be?

If not, you can largely blame your past EATING HABITS, as they are chiefly responsible for the way you feel and the way you look.

Let me urge you to resolve to keep in step with the times. Go modern! We demand the newest and best in our homes, our cars, our building and household equipment because they are beautiful to look at, dependable and efficient. YOU can have a THIS year's model body, too. Instead of remaining or permitting yourself to get aged, bent and stiff, a burden to yourself and others, it is easily possible to acquire the Vital Force, the Enduring Energy, the Sparkling Pep and Invigorating Good Health of YOUTH.

Then why tolerate an old-style, out-of-date body when you can be the owner of a Grade "A", FIRST CLASS one — by learning to eat delicious foods which have the power of revitalizing and renewing—MODERNIZING—every cell in your body?

Note from Elaine: Jack wrote *Your Health Cook Book* in 1954. Everyone thought he was crazy for preaching healthy eating habits. It has only been in the last one to two decades that we are realizing and embracing the idea that we are individually responsible for the way we feel and the way we look.

Growing up, I used to think cooking was complicated. Our midwestern meal mostly consisted of meat, potatoes, gravy, butter, and white bread. I remember setting the table with salt, pepper, butter, white bread, cream and sugar. Eventually, we added over cooked canned vegetables. And then there was always a dessert of cakes and pies made with lots of butter or lard. One of the first dinners I had with Jack, I realized cooking wasn't that complicated. In fact, it was simple, I couldn't believe it. He took three kinds of squash, zucchini, yellow and summer squash, chopped them up with some onions, bell peppers and mushrooms, then sauteed them. He added ground turkey seasoned with garlic and veggie seasoning from the health food store. It made my day as Jack would say, "Tastebuds dance with delight." My eating habits changed and so did my well being.

Below is a handout he gave at his lectures to show a few simple recipes.

LALANNE RECIPES

Potatoes La Lanne

1 medium potato
seasoning to taste (vegetable seasoning, garlic, and/or onion powder)
safflower oil

Pre-Heat broiler for 5 minutes. The slices should be placed on a foil covered cookie sheet.
Mix safflower oil and seasoning in a mixture, to taste.
Wash the potato with skin, carefully as though for baking, then dry. Slice potato crosswise in approximately 1/8-inch thickness, leaving skin on. Brush on or dip each slice in the mixture of oil and seasoning. Place each slice on the cookie sheet and broil for 3-5 minutes, until crispy brown. Flip the slices and brown the other side.
Can be served with a meal or as a substitute for potato chips.

Mashed Banana

1 ripe banana per serving
1 tsp. honey
1/2 tsp. lemon juice

Mash banana with a fork in a bowl. Add 1tsp. Honey, and 1/2tsp. Lemon juice.
Can be served in custard or compote form, and garnished with strawberries or fruit in season.

Blender Soup

1 can chicken broth or homemade chicken stock
1 carrot, Chopped
1 small bell pepper, chopped
1/2 zucchini, chopped
1 stalk celery, chopped
1/2 onion or 1 garlic clove

Mix the above ingredients in the blender. Pour in a saucepan and bring to a boil.
You may substitute any of the vegetables mentioned with other vegetables.

Variation #1
1 cup water
1/4 cup each (all chopped): celery, bell pepper, potato, cauliflower, carrots, cucumber, zucchini
1 clove garlic (optional)
Heat and serve as above.

BEFIT ENTERPRISES
430 Quintana Road, Morro Bay, CA 93442
Phone: (805) 772-6000 * Fax: (805) 772-2590 * Toll Free: 1-800-328-5225
Web Site: www.jacklalanne.com

Jack about to put Pototoes LaLanne
under the broiler.

Are You A Walking Billboard?

Think of yourself as a walking billboard. Does your billboard advertise, "I hate to exercise, I overeat, don't care how I look and feel?" It's never too late to change that billboard into "I obey nature's laws, I exercise regularly, eat sensibly, and I'm proud of the way I look and feel, because I made it happen."

I know that your measurements sort of sneak up on you in the course of a lifetime when you're preoccupied with work and raising a family, then suddenly your clothes are shrinking and that waistband is too tight. Your energy wanes and you don't feel as comfortable with yourself as usual. Isn't that a warning sign that maybe something should be done, something like an exercise program and a check on how and what you're eating?

Here's a few tips to consider:

- Above all, create an exercise routine habit.

- Instead of spreading butter or margarine on toast, using a small vegetable brush, lightly spread on some good vegetable oil and season. Add garlic powder for garlic bread.

- Don't eat if you aren't hungry.

- Don't snack between meals.

- Don't take in more calories than you're burning up.

- Broil instead of fry.

- Remove poultry skin when cooking chicken to save calories and fat.

- Don't salt your food until you've tasted it. It's an insult to the chef.

- Read contents of prepared food to detect hidden salt and sugar.

- If you have been in the habit of using excess salt, have your blood pressure monitored regularly.

- Reduce your sugar intake.

- Don't keep a secret cache of sweets around the house. You won't eat what you don't have.

"Don't exceed the feed limit." – LaLanne-ism

Josef Lavi The first time I met Jack was in 2001 in the office of Rick Hersh, his long-time agent, and Vice President of the William Morris Agency, for a meeting to promote our new invention, the Power Juicer. It later became the world-famous Jack LaLanne Power Juicer.

I have been blessed to be close to Jack and work with him for a decade. Jack was on a mission. He inspired me, as well as millions around the world, to change life for the better. He taught me about dedication to a mission, work ethic, and strong morals in order to accomplish our goals and to help others. One of the most important things I saw was Jack's love of people and how people loved Jack. When Jack decided to endorse the Power Juicer as his tool for juicing for life, he told me, "I have always believed in juicing. Young man, I will be there day and night to make sure that everyone around the world will know about my juicer and juicing as a way to health." Jack flew coast-to-coast to promote juicing, to shoot infomercials and give lectures to accomplish his goal of a juicer in every home.

During one of his trips to Florida, to promote the juicer on HSN, the juicer sold out earlier than expected, and we found we had the whole evening for ourselves. We asked Jack what he would like to do. Jack said, "Let's go for a good dinner and then to the club." Surprised, I looked at Lala and Lala looked at me, and we said, "Okay." So we went to dinner, and I started to take them back to the hotel, but then Jack said, "So which club are we going to?" I made a call to one of my friends to ask for an address for a club. When we walked in, the club was filled with a younger crowd of people. Before we knew it, Jack was surrounded with young men and women asking him questions, taking pictures, hugging him, and requesting autographs. Soon Lala was dancing with them, and before we knew it, we were all dancing.

Jack had his own unique way to come into people's hearts. He was an inspirational giant, and a great American icon. He was not only the Godfather of Fitness, he was a great father, husband, friend, and partner. Jack, we know that you are smiling and happy that your goal and mission is continuing.

Josef Lavi
Developer of the Jack LaLanne Power Juicer

Jack on Juicing

One of the expressions I have used when I am overly enthusiastic about something is, "When I play, I play for keeps and tear the grass in great big heaps!"

Sounds kind of silly doesn't it? However, if you analyze what I am trying to get across you will understand that when I do something, I do it with my mind, heart and soul for life! I don't deviate from my intended goal. It is important to first believe in your goal, believe that you can reach it, and then pursue to make it happen. I've done that with almost every phase of my life including juicing.

I have been asked so many times "Jack do you really juice? I see you on TV extolling the advantages of juicing." My answer to all of you who ask this question is YES. In fact, I have been juicing since I was a teenager; over seven decades. The first juicer I ever used was a press type. The fruits and vegetables had to be first ground up and put through a pressing machine. It was very antiquated and it was difficult to squeeze out all of the juice. It was in the era of the Ford Model T. Then a new generation of centrifugal juicers came on the market and I must have owned most of them, including a huge commercial one used in the health food stores. It stood more than 20 inches tall, measured 39 inches around and weighed sixty pounds. I still have that old juicer in what I call my museum of memorabilia. Today, with new, patented technology, juicers have more powerful, high output induction motors. This technique gives you less noise, more juice, less waste, and a wider opening. Thank goodness

we're not still driving Model T Fords and struggling with many of the old methods. We're living in this wonderful age where we have all these new inventions to help us to a better life.

I juice because a lot of the American diet consists of over-processed, overcooked foods. It's a known fact that we need five to six raw vegetables and four to five fresh fruits everyday. It seems that everything that we put into our body is cooked and I believe too much cooking kills a good deal of the nutrients. If you put live and vital foods in your body you're going to feel

On my 80th birthday, my wife Elaine, surprised me with a huge CARROT CAKE, made from the pulp of carrot, pineapple, and apple juice in the Jack LaLanne Power Juicer. It was fantastic and everyone loved it.

alive and vital. Your bloodstream is your "River of Life." Remember your 80 trillion cells feed and nourish your bloodstream. If that "River of Life" is polluted by unhealthy foods, your entire body will be adversely affected. Some people age prematurely because they have been on junk food diets and have polluted that "river." You might ask, "Why not get juice from a can or a bottle? It's too much trouble to cut up the fruit and vegetables and to clean the appliance." Not with today's technology! Canned and bottled drinks are often loaded with preservatives, salt, sugar, and artificial flavorings. Not with fresh juice. The nutrients of fresh juice go directly into your body. That's why many people say that they feel better after drinking them. A glass of fresh juice also appeases your hunger, keeps your energy up, and helps keep you clean inside.

Keith Mirchandani Jack was a hard-working California boy who almost single-handedly brought about the American fitness revolution. The original guru of total health and a true pioneer in the fitness and nutrition industry since he opened the first modern fitness center in 1936. He championed whole-body wellness in the 1950s — an unheard-of idea at that time.

I met Jack in 1995 and he became my dear friend. We collaborated for many years, marketing the Jack LaLanne Power Juicer, a tremendous success in the TV infomercial world. The Power Juicer helped launch the juicer category that is more popular than ever today: Jack's philosophy on life, fitness, food, and health is still relevant after all these years.

We even produced a short film about Jack called "The Godfather of Fitness" that premiered at the 2017 Tribeca Film Festival. Jack is truly the Godfather of Fitness, and I am honored to have known him. He was a friend, icon, and an inspiration to all of us here at Tristar Products.

Keith Mirchandani

Founder and CEO of Tristar Products, Inc. and the Executive Producer of "Godfather of Fitness."

Elaine's First Taste of Carrot Juice

Excerpt from *Total Juicing* by Elaine LaLanne and Richard Benyo, journalist, veteran distance runner, and former editor of *Runner's World* magazine.

When I met Jack in the 1950s, I was invited to his home for dinner. I noticed a huge metal contraption in the kitchen. It stood more than 20 inches high and it was really heavy. He said it was a juicer. I had never heard of a juicer before. He proceeded to

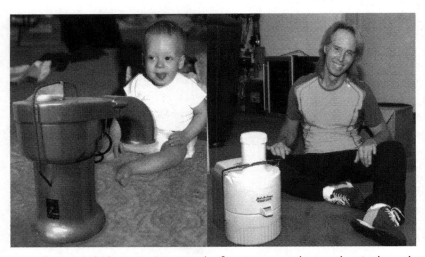

demonstrate how it worked. Selecting from a 25 pound bag of carrots, he quickly made a quart of carrot juice. I could not believe how sweet the juice was. He then added celery and other vegetables. He quickly made me a juice convert and I have been juicing all sorts of vegetables ever since.

Jon Allen, as a baby, sitting next to the first commercial juicer that Jack used.
Jon Allen, as an adult, sitting next to the first Jack LaLanne Power Juicer.

The Hollow Calorie

As mentioned, Jack would often write down a thought on anything he could find. Here are notes from an article he was going to write entitled "The Hollow Calorie."

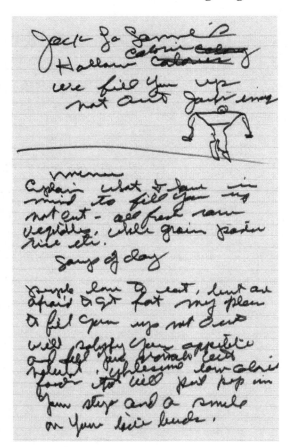

Jack LaLanne's Hollow Calorie

We fill you up, not out.

(Jack even drew a picture of himself – Jack's image.)

Menu

Explain what I have in mind to fill you up, not out – all fresh raw vegetables whole grain pasta rice, etc.

Soup of the Day

People love to eat, but are afraid to get fat. My plan to fill you up not out will satisfy your appetite and fill your stomach with natural unprocessed low calorie foods. It will put pep in your step and a smile on your taste buds!!!

Jack's Prediction

Even in the area of nutrition, Jack was a visionary. From his 1960 book "The Jack LaLanne Way to Vibrant Good Health," (page 143), Jack predicted, "Millions of words have been written on the subject of vitamins, minerals and food supplements. Hardly a month passes but some new discovery of the work of vitamins in preserving our health is reported by the press. Next, I predict it will be enzymes."

Jack on Drugs and Bodybuilding

"Your body is your most priceless possession, and the most pleasant thing in life is health." – Jack LaLanne

Today with the access of drugs, so many young bodybuilders are tempted to take the easy way out. When you start altering the hormonal balance of the body unnaturally, you are in for severe consequences. What we know about nutrition, we have nature's natural bodybuilding supplements. We know about vitamins and minerals. We also know about enzymes from natural sources by eating more natural whole grain products, more raw fruits and vegetables, and refraining from any processed food such as fats and sugars. With a solid nutrition plan, coupled with the supplements we know about, plus exercise, you can change so dramatically!

The body should be in perfect shape-in other words, good symmetry and without drugs. The use of unlawful drugs will destroy you mentally, physically, morally and spiritually. Drug users are only cheating and lying to themselves. They are also breaking the law as well as nature's law.

The movies in the 30's, 40's and 50's made weightlifters out to be clumsy, stupid freaks. Today, drugs and steroids actually do make the bodybuilders who use them look unnatural. Back then it was unheard of to use drugs; bodybuilders wanted to develop bodies that looked like Greek sculptures. The works of Phidias and Praxiteles were thought to be the best examples of perfection of proportion of the male human figure. Until the emphasis is put on symmetry and proportions you're not going to change this drug thing. As long as the judges continue to select winners on how huge somebody can be you're not going to solve this problem. It can only be solved if the judging standards are changed.

Education is also necessary. Bodybuilders have to be taught the harm they're doing to themselves and shown alternatives such as natural bodybuilding. Drug-free athletes have to be examples.

You must be a leader, not a follower. It takes discipline to stay away from drugs. You have to work a little harder, think more positively about getting better. But the rewards are greater. The real issue is responsibility. People have got to take responsibility for themselves and do something about it. They've got to have pride and discipline. God helps those who help themselves.

I'm proud of all you who are into natural bodybuilding. More and more bodybuilders are becoming aware of the pitfalls of steroids and growth-enhancing drugs. Today's drugs are causing emotional problems, aggressiveness, some intestinal removal, and even death. If you take drugs, it's like going to bed with a rattlesnake; it's got to get you!

SECTION FIVE

Humor, Faith & Successful Aging

Jack was the master of creating iconic humorous quips and motivating quotes to empower us into seeing ourselves as fit and healthy and believing we could make and sustain a healthy lifestyle.

Dan Isaacson
Former director of California Governor's Council on Physical Fitness,
President of Isaacson Fitness, LLC, public speaker

Jack on Humor

Without a sense of humor, it's practically impossible to be happy. Without a sense of humor, you'll have a tough time having friends. Who wants to be around a "down-in-the-mouth" sour puss? Laughter is the greatest medicine known to man. This has been proven time and time again by top, leading doctors, psychologists and psychiatrists. The condition that the world has always been in, if we took it seriously we'd go nuts. We have to look at the bright, happy and cheerful side of life. Don't take ourselves too seriously. One of the prime prerequisites for a sense of humor is a healthy and disease-free body. It's difficult to laugh and be happy when you're sick and ailing. So health (physical and mental) are a must for a merry, long life. Laugh and the world laughs with you; cry and you cry alone.

Jack's Quips

"There's nothing I wouldn't do for my wife, there's nothing she wouldn't do for me. So, we spend our lives doing nothing for each other." Jack quipped to Keith Morrison during a *Dateline* interview.

I've never told my stomach I'm a poor man.

The only thing good about a donut is the hole in the middle.

I'd hate to wake up in the morning and find myself dead.

Henry Ford got people off their feet and onto their seat. I want to get people off their seat and onto their feet.

My wife likes to run. Run up my bills and run off at the mouth.

Elaine: If you do more feats of strength, I'll divorce you.
Jack: Promise?

Elaine: I'll be there shortly!
Jack: I'll be there longley.

Fan: Mr. LaLanne, it's nice to meet you!
Jack: Mr. LaLanne couldn't make it. Jack came in his place!

Fan: Hi Jack! I used to watch you!
Jack: Now I'm watching you!!

Fan: How did you pull all those boats?
Jack: I just do the best I can with the equipment I have.

Elaine: Do you mind if we leave a little early?
Jack: It's mind over matter. If you don't have a mind, it doesn't matter.

Reporter: What is the best advice you can give on eating out?
Jack: Don't exceed the feed limit!

Fan at the airport: Hi Jack!
Jack with a twinkle in his eye: Don't greet me like that on an airplane!

After completing the 70 boat feat, a reporter asked Jack what he planned to do for his 80th birthday. I'm going to tow my wife across the bathtub!

Jack, on one of his TV shows, explaining an exercise: **Sit on the edge of your chair, hands on each side of the seat, bring both knees or one knee into the chest trying to touch your forehead. If you can touch your forehead, you've got a long forehead!**

Reporter: Do you really like to exercise?
Jack: **I hate to exercise but I like the results.**

During an interview with Steve Downs from *Natural Bodybuilding* magazine (Feb 1996 p. 38) when asked, how old are you?
Jack: **I'm one day younger than I was yesterday!**

Jack during a lecture: **I'm going to live to be 150 and I want you to stick around and find out!**

In a newspaper article before one of Jack's swims, a reporter asked how he felt.
Jack said, **I'm as nervous as a June bride that's pregnant.**

Jack on Phil Donahue TVshow with Linus Pauling:
Linus you've received many awards including the Nobel Peace Prize for Vitamin C. I've won one, too. The No Belly Prize!

Walking out of Barnaby's Restaurant with Jack, a customer in a confused look pointed at Jack and said, "I know you?" Jack shook his hand and quipped,
Hi, I'm Richard Simmons, do you want to work out with me tomorrow at six in the morning?

Jack had a sense of humor to go with his goal to make everyone healthy and happy.

Don Jung
CPA, and author of "Rockin' Through Troubled Waters"

Oops! Jack Asked The Wrong Question

One night while I was in Paris, I went to dinner at a very high-class restaurant called Maxim's. Whenever I go into any restaurant I'm not familiar with, I like to be sure all the food is fresh. I have pretty high standards, you see. Well, when the waiter came over to our table, I asked him if the fish was fresh. In a loud, indignant voice, which could be heard by everyone in the restaurant, he replied, **"Monsieur! Everything in Maxim's is FRRRRRRREEESH!"** I didn't say a word after that.

Dan Isaacson It was at the Governor's Council on Physical Fitness and Sports where I met Jack. I excitedly walked up to him, shook his hand, he patted me on the shoulder, and with a twinkle in his eye, laughingly said, "What do you want to tell me that I don't want to know!"

At one of our meetings while addressing the Governor's Council, Jack came to the stage for his report, put his arms on the podium, paused, and looked out at his audience with everyone ready for his motivating presentation. He gazed at the crowd as if to gain his composure for his speech and then surprised everyone as he slammed his fists on the top of the podium and said, "Wake up, sit up, tighten your abs, shoulders back and look like you're the experts in health and fitness you're supposed to be. You're the leader, so look and act like it!" I've never seen an entire crowd of PhD's, MD's and the top health experts in the State of California move so fast and everyone did exactly as he directed! Only Jack could get away with it, he always seemed to have a twinkle in his eye.

John Cates, Peter Vidmar, Olympian gymnast, and Jack.

Dan Isaacson
Former Director of California Governor's Council on Physical Fitness,
President of Isaacson Fitness, LLC, public speaker

John Cates During a meeting of the California Governor's Council on Physical Fitness and Sports, John asked the Council members on stage to report on how they had promoted the importance of health and fitness since the last Council meeting. When it was Jack's turn to report, Peter Vidmar, jokingly pressed to a straight arm, straight leg handstand on top of the table, and said he was going to hold this position during Jack's entire presentation. Knowing that Jack and LaLa always had the most to report, he knew he was in for a long handstand. Both Jack's report and Peter's handstand were unbelievable. The Council meetings were always productive as well as entertaining. What a great dedicated council.

John Cates
Former Executive Director of the President's Council on Physical Fitness and Sports,
Former Executive Director of California Governor's Council on Physical Fitness and Sports

Tony Little My favorite memories about Jack are when we worked at HSN (Home Shopping Network). While waiting in between appearances, he would come down the hall from his dressing room to the greenroom and we'd just talk. He would tell me little things that made me laugh all the time. One of my favorites was when he said, "Tony, I make love to my wife, Elaine, nearly every day. Nearly on Monday, nearly on Tuesday and almost on Wednesday." That was just his personality. I remember Elaine always being with him. She was like the partner you wanted in your life, always with you, always believes in you, always loves you no matter what you're doing. She just had the personality of being the biggest supporter for that guy of any wife I've ever seen in my life.

Tony Little
Certified Personal Trainer, Physical Fitness Specialist and
former National Bodybuilding Champion, HSN spokesperson

Reflection from Elaine

On July 17, 2000, Jack was honored to be Larry's guest for the entire hour. As we walked into the studio in Hollywood, we expected to see many production people but it was just Larry who welcomed us as old friends and showed us around. Entering the studio area we noticed that the cameras were locked off remotely with no operators and no one else present except Larry, Jack, our son Dan, and me for the entire hour. A very intimate setting! Jack's one-liner while being interviewed by Larry King: **"Larry don't interrupt while I'm interrupting,"** was so Jack! January 23, 2021, Larry King left us to go onto the next expression of his life, 10 years to the day that my loving husband, Jack passed away. When he was home, Jack never missed an episode of the Larry King Show.

Nico Saad While staying at my house in Ensenada in the early 60's, Jack was working out on the patio very early in the morning. My mother, Juanita, came running to me worried and upset and cried out, **"Something is wrong with your friend, he's breathing hard, yelling, and jumping up and down."** Not only was Jack a great friend all those years but a great inspiration to me.

Nico Saad
Federal and State Director of Tourism in Baja California and
owner of the San Nicolas Resort Hotel and Casino in Ensenada, Mexico

Per Hanson Jack had many one-liners and of course a lot of energy. A lot of times people asked him, "How old are you going to be?" Jack's answer, **"I don't care if I die tomorrow as long as I feel good."** Another question Jack was asked, "If you work out do you have to do that for the rest of your life?" His answer, **"Do you stop brushing your teeth?"**

Per Hanson
Golf Pro, Bastad Golfklubb, Bastad, Sweden

Francene Green-Litteral I was 15 years old in the summer of 1960, and my friends and I spent many days at the beach. When my friends would pick me up, I had to navigate my way around my mother to get to the front door. It was nothing new. My mother would exercise almost every day with this "Jack" guy on TV. She had a beach towel on the floor, a kitchen chair next to the towel, and a long rubbery stretchy thing she called her "Glamour" something, and it was tied around our front door handle. Little did I know, 23 years later, I would be working with and for Jack LaLanne and his wife Elaine. When I introduced my mother to Jack and Elaine, she was stunned and speechless! Jack simply replied, "I spent a lot of time on the floor with your mother!"

Francene Green-Litteral
Former Pepperidge Farm franchise owner
Designer of Jack LaLanne Bread and Cereal products

Jerry Kahn I met Jack LaLanne in 1953 while working at the popular Bert Goodrich Gym in Hollywood where many bodybuilders and movie stars worked out. Jack would often drop by to say hello to Bert.

I'm a guy about 5'6". I thought you had to be tall to look like a bodybuilder. I was surprised to find Jack was about my height and had an outstanding body that made me realize you don't have to be six feet tall to obtain strength, health and muscles. Meeting Jack had a big influence and impact on me to pursue my goal in the health and fitness industry.

Because of Jack, I set a goal of building Holiday Health and Fitness locations in the Eastern states and added four new Holiday Spas locations in Orange County. Jack at that time was a national TV celebrity and each day he would do a live show on a local station and then send it to stations throughout the country.

One day he invited me to the TV studio in Hollywood. I thought he was making a commercial. Picture this! Thinking it was to be a TV commercial I wore my best custom suit, shirt, and tie, plus my new heavy wingtip leather shoes. After arriving, I found myself on his live TV show which was not scripted.

During my segment after a short interview, I found myself lying on the floor, lifting my legs up and down, rolling over and doing pushups. "Ok! Stand up! Let's get that old heart beating," Jack prompted.

While Jack kept prompting his viewers to lift their legs higher and higher, I too, was lifting my legs higher and higher with sweat dripping lower and lower. The bright hot lights didn't help either. After the segment was over, I looked like someone had dumped a bucket of water on my head! Jack looked as if he had just taken a casual stroll in the park dressed in his usual lightweight jumpsuit and ballet shoes. Moral of the story, ask for details!

Jack was always fun to be with. He had a beautiful singing voice, inspired millions and was mainly a true great friend.

Jerry Kahn
Founder of the Holiday Health Spas.

Happy's Joke Book

Jack had a great sense of humor and loved jokes. Here's Jack and Happy on his show posing with their joke book. From time to time, Jack would spontaneously stop an exercise and tell a corny joke or pun. When the crew responded with jeers, he would blame it on Happy. It was a big hit with his viewers and the jokes came pouring in.

Here are some of Jack's and Happy's favorites

The first day of school, the kindergarten teacher told her class, "If anyone has to go to the bathroom, hold up two fingers." After a quiet moment, one little boy asked, "How's that gonna help?"

A taxpayer wrote to his State Controller to confess that he'd cheated on his income taxes ten years ago, and hadn't been able to get a good night's sleep since. He enclosed $25.00 and this note, "If I still can't sleep, I'll send you the balance."

Thanks to the Interstate Highway System it is now possible to travel across the country from coast to coast without seeing anything.

My son is only 3 and he can spell his name forward and backward! What's his name? OTTO!

A major cigarette company was looking for a spokesperson who could counteract all the negativity about smoking. So they put an ad in the paper looking for a senior citizen who smoked and was still in good health despite an advanced age. They found the perfect person. He was a spry, 89-year old man who smoked 3 packs of cigarettes a day. The cigarette executives immediately rushed to sign him up. When they arrived at his house, he was just as described: alert, perky and extremely animated. They didn't waste any time asking him to be their spokesman and offered him an immense salary to speak for their company. The old man agreed and immediately signed a contract to appear as their spokesperson As they were telling him filming would begin at 10:00 AM but he must be at the studio at 6 AM for makeup and rehearsal. He looked at the cigarette executives and bellowed, *6 AM! I don't stop coughin' till 11:15!*

Faith

Faith is Trusting and Believing

I believe that having faith is a part of any self-improvement program. Even having faith is discipline. There has to be an omnipotent power that puts everything together. As Elaine often says, "This omnipotent power is in us, around us and through us. Nature shows us this every day of our lives."

On the set with Happy. Jack asked Happy to say his prayers.

Having faith reminds me of a little story I often tell in my lectures. Johnny was a little kid whose goal was to win a race at school. He participated in every race but was always dead last. The final race of the season was in progress and, as usual, Johnny was running last. All of a sudden, halfway, he began to run faster and faster. He passed one, then another and another and pretty soon he was in front and he won the race!

His coach said, "I can't believe it Johnny, I can't believe it! I saw you talking to yourself out there, what were you saying?"

Johnny answered, "I wasn't talking to myself, I was talking to God."

The coach asked, "What were you saying to God?"

Johnny replied, "Dear God you lift my legs and I'll put them down, dear God. You lift my legs up and I'll put them down."

We all need a little help from time to time. You cannot be in my profession of physical fitness (connected with the mind and the body) and not believe that there is a supreme that keeps this universe together.

We are Wonderfully and Fearfully Made

Even with all the technology today, scientists are still exploring human anatomy; how to make a calculator like our brain or a pumping system like our heart. The heart is an indestructible muscle except when circulation going to the heart is impaired. Do you think that humans could ever devise a filtering system like our kidneys or a laboratory like our liver? Do you think that science could ever make a machine that can be damaged only by a lack of use? Do you think that we could ever create a machine that changes constantly like the seventy trillion cells in the body which keep changing (except the central nervous system). Hence, if you exercise and put the right fuel in your body it helps to reverse the aging process. Yes! "We are wonderfully and fearfully made!"

Great Things in Life

We should live the life we have vibrantly and in good health. This, without question, involves the awareness of a creator, no matter how we conceive it. It means spiritual exercises -- prayer and meditation--for the development of our inner selves as well as deeper thought on this wonderful life and body we have been given. Our bodies are truly God's living temple but how many of us treat it reverently? Too many of us take it for granted.

The way I see it, two great things in life are feeling well and looking well. Two additional things are vitamins F and G: Faith and God. Without them nothing positive is going to happen in our lives. We need faith in something, whether it be faith in God or faith in oneself. I want to reemphasize the three fold nature of the LaLanne program:

- Nourish the body through wise nutrition and exercise
- Nourish the mind through intellectual activity, reading, listening and observing.
- Nourish the spirit through prayer and meditation.

Why shouldn't prayers be an integral part of a program to build health and vitality? It was the "faith of our forebears" that is credited with building this great nation out of the confusion and conflict of its beginnings. The great and wise founding fathers were not reluctant to ask for help and guidance. Neither were the wonderful men and women who pushed on across the continent in covered wagons to fulfill the infant nation's destiny. George Washington often sought divine guidance when the job seemed beyond his mortal powers. Abraham Lincoln, though a communicant of no formal religious congregation, frankly went to his knees when perplexities all but overwhelmed him.

Have Faith to Overcome Fear

In a television interview, a famous director was asked about fear. Particularly, the fear of failure in expensive undertakings. His comment was that, of course, he knew fear. He went on to say that most good actors "suffer" a fear of failure before going on stage. Star athletes feel the same fear before the bell rings or the ball is kicked off. Fear is one harmful factor at work for all of us. As we age, it seems to get easier to fear more things.

I remember how it was in the Great Depression when men and women lost their jobs. They sat moping and worrying. You could almost see them age. Men of 35 and 40 became old overnight. Their hair seemed to turn gray faster, lines appeared in their faces, their shoulders sagged. They lacked the confidence to seek the few jobs that were open. Franklin D. Roosevelt, a great man who had overcome emotional and physical handicaps himself, reminded the nation, "All we have to fear is fear itself." You can believe that he knew how to use prayer in his life.

There are ways of overcoming fear and other crippling states of mind. You have to find your own way. There are many entrances to your faith and each faith has its own door. Obviously we will all come to the day when we'll pass on to our next expression of life. While we're here, why not make the most of it?

Banish fear, frustration, and worry. Gain energy by doing. Learn to relax, nap, and find peace of mind. We need faith to overcome fear.

Successful Aging

"People don't die of old age, they die of neglect and inactivity." - *Jack LaLanne*

A survey was made on 100 people who were in their 100's to find out secrets of their long, healthy life. They were interviewed in depth; most were very vigorous, happy and productive, had hobbies and were moderate in most everything they did. After months and months of time, energy and money spent to find out their formula for a great life, here are the findings--so simple you will be amazed:

a. a high self-esteem

b. a sense of humor

c. a strong desire to live

Are you as surprised at the findings as I was? Were you expecting a secret food or drink or a special exercise?

When you slow down too much, you come to a stop.

I'm not going to say that you can take a ninety-year old woman and make her look like a sixteen-year old girl, but with good eating habits, a good exercise program and a good attitude, she can be the sexiest, healthiest ninety-year old woman you've ever seen. And that's what counts!

Believe me, I know people who died at 40 and were buried at 70. I don't care how long I live, I want to LIVE while I'm living. In my lectures, I always tell my students that, "I'd rather wear out than rust out." I really mean it!

The aging process begins the moment we're born, but it's exciting to know that as you're reading this, millions of your body's 70 trillion cells are dying and new ones are taking their places. So if you improve your eating and exercise habits, those new cells should be superior to the old ones, right? That means you COULD be a new you!

You're never too old to begin taking care of your body. However, before you begin any exercise program, get a check up by your medical doctor. When he or she says go ahead, then go ahead with enthusiasm!

Now, what kind of food are you ingesting? Are you eating live and vital foods? The slower you eat, the less you eat. So chew each mouthful at least 15 times. Savor every delicious bite and think good thoughts like, "This is going to make my waistline firmer," or "this mouthful will help my sex life," or "my new diet is improving my elimination."

A scientific exercise and nutrition program will help give you more strength and energy. You'll look and feel better. You'll probably find that you sleep more soundly, digest food better, and some of your minor aches and pains might even be alleviated. *All you have to do is put your mind to it!*

Mind and body go hand-in-hand. No physical accomplishment is possible without full cooperation of your mind. Along with a healthy mind, you need a healthy body, created by proper nutrition, regular, safe exercise and discipline.

Build Your Health Account

Since you've eaten the same way all your life, tackle one dietary change at a time. Instead of over-cooking vegetables, under cook them; instead of white bread, try whole wheat; rather than red meat, try chicken or fish. Don't fry foods, broil them; substitute garlic or onion powder for salt. Invent new, healthy recipes, and take a scientifically planned vitamin and mineral supplement to help ward off the aging process.

Build up your "health account." My wife, Elaine and I treat our health account just like our bank accounts. If you don't put anything in you can't take anything out. You have to earn the right to enjoy an occasional cocktail or dessert. It isn't what you do once in a while that counts, it's what you do ALL of the time that counts.

Older people don't feel old unless they're told they're old. That's why mandatory retirement is a killer. God didn't set any age at which we have to slow down. SO DON'T DO IT! Many of my friends became rich and famous with careers they started during their so-called "senior" years. So don't be bored. Or boring! Find a hobby. Maybe it's gardening or golfing or artwork. Swimming or horse-back riding. Folk or ballroom dancing. Start school. Open your own business. Get off your butt. Do something!

The human body is a miracle of resiliency. No matter what your age or physical condition, you can always improve the way it works. Muscles, like your mind, get weak with inactivity, so strengthen them with exercise. And since flexibility depends upon the condition of your ligaments and tendons, help them maintain elasticity by stretching. People don't die of old age, they die of neglect. If I can help you do things you haven't done for years, I've helped you delay the aging process, haven't I? So begin an exercise program today. Start slowly. Be careful. And, be inspired knowing that as you read this, people in their eighties and nineties are happily swimming, lifting weights and jogging for the fun and good health of it.

Lazy Retirement versus Active Retirement

I have lived so long I have known literally hundreds of individuals who have retired. Some in their late 40s or early 50s. Unless you find another interest, retirement is getting up and going to bed with eating and television in between. Statistics indicate that most men who retire die within five years of retiring. Not good odds, is it? A good retirement, to me, is about two weeks.

We must all have an active interest in life. Stagnating on the couch watching game shows on TV is not the way to go. Besides, this type of lazy retirement ruins that jubilant Friday afternoon feeling. The exaltation of the weekend is never to be felt again. The only people who really enjoy their retirement are those who have an all-encompassing interest that substitutes totally for their time spent in the workforce. Even so there's a big difference.

As a retiree, unlike when you were working at the office, it isn't mandatory for anyone to listen to you any more. That alone can lessen your sense of importance. You may even feel that you have no purpose in the machinations of society.

I have known scores of people who have been utterly excited over the prospect of retiring. "Now I can travel." "Now I'll have time with my family." "Now I can clean my teeth after every meal." But what happens after a few months? They start missing being at work. I have known gym owners who have rushed to reopen within a couple of years of retiring. One 64-year-old publisher, after selling his fitness magazine, couldn't bear staying at home with nothing to do. A year later he was back into publishing. Why? "I miss it!" he told me. "But you were always grumbling about the price of paper, the problems with staff and freelance writers," I said. "I know, I know," he replied. "But I missed all of that, too."

One solution to dodging full retirement is to retire partially. Some people find that taking a two- or three-day-a-week job suits them just fine. They feel useful, get out of the house, earn some cash and yet still have time for enjoying freedom they can't experience when locked into a full-time vocation.

How is your current job? Are you stressed at the abundance of work? Frustrated with fellow staff members? Is your commute too stressful and time consuming? Remember we only have one life, and believe me it's a happy day when you actually enjoy your work. What better reward is there than to know that what you are doing is helping people live longer, and enjoy their lives to the fullest. It's mind blowing.

Living a Positive Lifestyle

You know what? You and I, we should get up in the morning and we should say "Hallelujah!" Thank God that we're alive and that we're living in this moment. What we have learned about physical fitness, about nutrition, about vitamins, about minerals, about exercise and how it's never too late to be born again. We can't separate the mind and the body. These are all wonderful, wonderful things. You and I have these tools to help us to have a better life.

Thoughts are things. Negativity is what kills you. It's tough to do, but you've got to work at living. Most people work at dying, but anybody can die; the easiest thing on this earth is to die. But to live takes guts, it takes energy, vitality, it takes thought. We have so many negative influences out there that are pulling us down. You've got to be strong to overcome these adversities. That's why I never stop.

Sex Life - Keeping it Alive and Well

When the subject of my health and fitness seminars turns to sex, there is always a man in the audience who asks, "Jack, can I overdo it?" My answer is always the same, "TRY IT!"

Sex is a result of what you have in your brain: your imagination, your fantasies. Without them your sex life could become hum-drum.

You have to have energy. You have to be in shape for it. It takes vitality. It takes enthusiasm. And there are a great number of people who don't have enough of either to make sex all that it can be.

A man's sex drive can rapidly diminish due to lack of exercise and proper nutrition. If a woman's sexual appetite begins to disappear, she might assume that she's not in love anymore, or that she's getting too old. Not so! You can still enjoy an exciting sex life. It's what you put into it. Your physical condition, a positive mental outlook, and self-esteem all come into play.

SO, FOR SEX'S SAKE, EXERCISE!! Work those hips, thighs, chest and buttocks. Tighten up what needs tightening. For years I've advocated strong, firm, healthy bodies.

Don't discount your nutrition either. Foods, in their natural state, bursting with nutrients that are low in fat, high in nutrition and full of vitamins and minerals, help build up your health and energy. So it doesn't stand to reason that the more energy you have the better the sex.

On my 70th birthday, while handcuffed and feet-shackled (throw in some strong winds and water currents), I towed seventy boats with seventy people a mile and a half through Long Beach Harbor. Everyone thought it was impossible. Everyone but me! Surely, if I can accomplish that feat at seventy, a man half my age should be able to keep afloat in the bedroom for a few minutes. With good health and a bit of imagination, you can make your sex life great!

SECTION SIX

Family Scrapbook Memoirs

Dr. Yvonne LaLanne Dad was notorious rather than famous. I struggled to explain what he did for a living. Physical Culturist? Because he was my dad he was the best, the most, and the finest dad in the world. He walked on his hands and could beat up any dad on the block. By the time I was a teenager, he was well known due to the ubiquity of the TV show. But he was still just my dad, and as such, he was sometimes annoying.

When I lived at home and they did a live show every day, he would try out the joke of the day on me. If I groaned and rolled my eyes, he used that joke. If I laughed, he would find another joke. I remember how he used to light my cigarette for me. Dad would never tell anyone how to live and never criticize or shame a person for their lifestyle choices, unless he was asked. Instead he would simply light my cigarettes for me. Clarence Budington Kelland said, "My father didn't tell me how to live. He lived and let me watch him do it." This was my father. I should mention, I am no longer a smoker.

The greatest impact his life's work had on me was I never developed a sweet tooth/sugar addiction that had adversely changed the health of most Americans. I internalized the benefits of exercise. I became a doctor of Chiropractic. I had a VERY famous last name.

My dad's legacy is that he normalized the idea that everyone should be on the exercise band wagon. He started housewives exercising, which caught the attention of their kids, and the rest is history. He was loyal, focused and dedicated. He will be forever remembered for that.

Dr. Yvonne LaLanne

Chiropractor

Dan Doyle LaLanne My mother was an on-air personality on ABC in San Francisco. She was the co-host of The Les Malloy Show which aired from 4:30 to 6 pm everyday which consisted of a 12- piece orchestra, interviews, and entertainment. I even remember seeing Johnny Mathis and Phyllis Diller on the show from time to time.

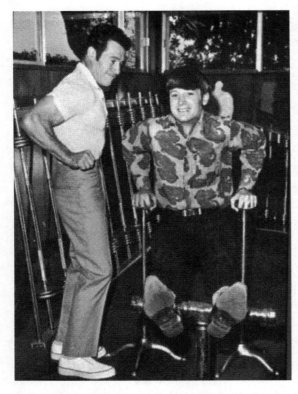

Jack and Danny. Danny using Jack's hand balancing pedestals with feet prompted up on the T-Bar. Jack used the T-bar to anchor his body when he was lifting heavy weights to stabilize his lower body. The T-bar was anchored to the ground. In the background are the fixed weight barbells in different weights. They were all chrome plated.

My mother met Jack after booking him for the show to do pushups nonstop for 90 minutes. In 1951, ABC executives asked him to put together a half-hour exercise show. After several years, they ultimately dated and after a long courtship got married.

I remember the first time Jack came to our house, he insisted on making dinner and brought all the fixins, including an extra-long loaf of white sourdough bread. The first thing he did was scrape all the white part off the crust, rolled it in a ball, and said to me before dinner, "Come on son, let's go outside and play some catch." I grabbed my Rawlings Mitt and hardball and headed out onto the street. As we were throwing the ball back and forth, Jack picked up the rolled-up ball of french bread and threw the fastest ball I had ever seen, hitting me right in the solar plexus. I was stunned for a moment and said, "I thought that was going to be part of our fancy dinner." Jack said "No, the white part is no good for you. The only part we are eating is the toasted crust. That is the best part!"

Several other memories stand out. Jack was an enthusiastic waterskier. He had a small Owens cabin cruiser he used for water skiing. We would often go out under the Bay Bridge that spans from San Francisco to Oakland. I swallowed a lot of saltwater trying to learn to ski behind that cabin cruiser. We also fished under the Golden Gate bridge and he brought our catch to a fantastic Chinese restaurant where I learned to like seaweed soup and other Chinese delicacies. This was my first encounter with healthy food, and it definitely made an impression on me. In school the kids would tease me stating that healthy food tastes horrible and other comments. I would respond with "It's not the food, it's how it is prepared." That is one of my first memories of Jack LaLanne.

Jack was enthusiastic, truthful and a preacher. His legacy is all around us. Health and fitness clubs, exercise shows, protein drinks, food supplements, stretch bands, and exercise equipment. We still have the original equipment he invented and own hundreds of his half-hour shows. He influenced many of the baby boomers that watched with their parents and then grew up to create the very ideals he had been preaching in the generation before.

Dan Doyle LaLanne
Professional Forensic Photographer

Jon LaLanne Have you ever heard the expression, "The light came on?" I well remember when it happened to me. I was taking harmonica lessons and it came to a point that it just got too complicated. I was going to quit, but something inside me said, "That's what you always do! Your Dad would never quit." Dad was always talking about perseverance, and never giving up. So, I decided to finally apply myself and do the frustrating work that was necessary. A couple of months later, I was in an underground parking garage. As I was getting out of the car, a light came on. "I picked up the harmonica, and started playing. This time it was different. For some reason the complicated notes and scales I had practiced for months, started to connect. The muscle memory repetition training Dad

spoke of was coming out in the form of the blues. When I was done I heard a loud echoing clap-clap-clap beyond the cars. A man in the garage was listening, unbeknownst to me. He absolutely loved it! It was at this particular moment, I knew I had arrived on the other side. Eventually, like Dad, I became obsessed with practice. I eventually became a professional harmonica player, singer and songwriter. However, today, I make custom surfboards, which is an even more compelling and complicated example of perseverance and practice; but that's another book.

The first time I realized Dad's impact on the world was, unfortunately, after he passed. I attended amazing trade shows, like IDEA, with Mom. Fans would come up to our Jack LaLanne Memorabilia booth and tell their stories of life-changing transformations they experienced, all because of Dad. The brightness in their eyes shone on me and then it hit me. Dad was Tony Robbins before Tony Robbins ever made a speech. Not only did Dad teach health and fitness, but he taught self-reliance, self-improvement, and personal responsibility to inspire others. He preached, "You can't take care of anybody else unless you take care of yourself first." Many people I talked to at these conventions were in dark places. Dad inspired them to take action for the better and it was possible to make the change. One gentleman came all the way from Mongolia to present Mom with a beautiful gold-plated dish in appreciation of how Dad had inspired him. Another man and his daughter brought grapefruits to our booth from a tree Dad had planted in our old place in Palm Springs. I never got to see the fruit of that tree until the trade show. That was a real tearjerker for me. The last 10 years of doing these trade shows has even given me new insight as to how Dad impacted the world.

Today I play the harmonica whenever asked but I am a surfboard designer, shaper, and maker. My friend Bob Hurley, a former surf board shaper and manufacturer, sold his business to NIKE. A friend of mine in Australia sent me photos of the new Bob Hurley design of "Hurley brand clothing," a hi-tech surfing, skateboarding and training center that just opened down the street from him. He said, "I'm sure your Dad had something to do with this new training center!" I thought for a moment and said to myself, "He's right." There are gyms and training centers across the globe. Dad's dream and mission has indeed come true.

Along with gym equipment, many of the "gizmos" we see on television today, such as stretch bands and protein drinks, Dad came out with decades prior. Often, while watching TV, and another one of these new devices comes on Mom will mention, "Jack invented that back in the 1950's." Dad's legacy continues to live on.

Jon LaLanne

Surfboard designer, shaper and make, professional harmonica player and musician

Lora LaLanne As I was sitting on the floor, after opening a Christmas present of one of Jack's books, I looked up at him and asked, "What could I do to tighten my stomach and build up my chest?" He lit up like the Christmas tree and immediately gave me a series of exercises to do. To this day I still do them.

If you asked him a question he told you like it was! He loved to talk about exercise and nutrition, never missed a workout and never deviated from his eating habits. When going out to dinner I noticed his discipline especially when eating. Never would he have a piece of cake or desert, he would have a piece of fresh fruit. I can still hear him saying "Don't exceed the feed limit."

He was no fake, he was real. I never ever saw him down in the dumps or gloomy. He was always positive and always looked on the bright side of everything.

A veteran of WWII, he was a real patriot, and cared about our country and our flag. He was serious, funny, and dedicated.

He didn't seem interested in nor talked about money. He was more about helping people to help themselves.

He was classy. He didn't care if you were rich or poor, he treated everyone the same. He had a beautiful singing voice and would often sing at our family parties. Even in a restaurant if he found out someone was having a birthday he would go over and sing to them. He was a good dancer too.

Jack was so sincere when he talked, and he really walked the walk. He not only exercised the body, but the mind and soul of every American he inspired.

Lora LaLanne
Wife of Jon LaLanne

Tom LaLanne On Christmas day, 1952, Jack had me on his television show, doing push ups and jumping jacks. I was 5. Not everyone has a famous uncle with his own TV show. I was impressed by his enthusiasm for his work, and by everyone around him. As I grew up, Jack became more and more famous. I was exceptionally proud of him, but didn't really relate to all of the buzz around him. Jack was just my dad's brother-- my uncle. Of all of the famous people I have met, Jack was probably the most down to earth. His show was so popular with people, mostly housewives, because he had this amazing demeanor about him. People thought he was talking directly to them as individuals. And the amazing thing was that he was. Jack was just being himself on his TV show, and he was no different in real life.

As I grew older, I realized that Jack's importance in the world of health grew exponentially. Everyone knew who he was, and what he stood for. Even Jack acknowledged that early in his life, a lot of people thought he was crazy. But the world finally caught up to Jack. He used to preach that anything in life is possible, and you can make it happen. Also, unlike a lot of his contemporaries in the physical fitness world, Jack was easily as interested in diet as he was in exercise.

Jack's influence on my life was substantial. From an early age, I understood how and what to eat, and the value of exercise in keeping and staying healthy. I owe him a lot. I was blessed to know Jack, and to grow up in his shadow.

I have a lot of Jack stories, but this one might be my favorite. It was 1967, and I had just returned to California from Army basic training at Fort Benning, Georgia. I flew home to Los Angeles to see my then-girlfriend, Jackie, and now my wife of 50 years. I arrived at Jack and Elaine's home in Hollywood late at night, after they had gone to bed. The next morning, I got up and went to the kitchen to talk to Hattie, their long-term housekeeper and huge part of the LaLanne family. Hattie told me that Jack wanted me to come down to the studio to see him shooting his daily show. He left the keys to his new Cadillac El Dorado with instructions for me to drive into the studio parking lot where I would be met by the lot guard. I met the guard, who pointed to a door, and told me to walk in. Somehow, I thought I would be away from the action, where I could watch the show. It turned out that the door opened directly onto the stage where Jack was taping his national TV show. Jack saw me, and announced to the cameras that his nephew Tommy had just walked in, and he wanted to talk to me on the show. I was wearing jeans and a t-shirt, but my most important feature was my haircut – a very short buzz-cut from basic training. That haircut would be entirely acceptable today, but not in 1967. Jack summoned me to center stage, introduced me, told the camera that I had just returned from basic training. He then proceeded to question me for 10 minutes or so on my Army service, the U.S. military in general. To say that I was unprepared for that experience would be an understatement. I survived this somewhat embarrassing situation, but didn't realize that it would also be shared with most of my college fraternity brothers. It seems as if half of their mothers had watched the show, and passed their reports on to their sons. As you can imagine, it took me a while to live that one down. I have to say that Jack was proud and supportive of me, and only wanted to share my experiences with his audience, but I wasn't so pleased with the experience at the time. As I look back on it, I have to say that I am now amused.

Jack's legacy is his stamp on the whole health industry. As I said above, late in his life, Jack was considered the godfather of the health industry, when all of his views about nutrition and exercise were not only accepted, but treated as "THE TRUTH."

3 Words (actually 4): One of a Kind. As my dad used to say, they threw away the mold with Jack. It is hard to believe there will ever be another person who is as charismatic and influential on other people as Jack has been when it comes to their health.

Tom LaLanne
Attorney and Nephew of Jack

Susan LaLanne Growing up with the last name LaLanne, I was somehow always considered to be a choice for athletic ability when vying for a spot on any sports team. I was not always the best, but thankful for the opportunity to try to live up to expectations. After living half of my life (I am now 77) I became very interested in swimming. Living in Kona, Hawaii, I have had the pleasure of swimming in the warm ocean and spent time long distance swimming. I decided to compete in an Alcatraz swim because Jack did it, and I could, too. After about a year of training, I entered a Sharkfest Alcatraz swim and won 1st place in my age group. I did the swim with a wetsuit and cannot imagine how the real good swimmers do the event almost buck naked, like my swimmer nephew, Chris LaLanne. This event inspired me to train and swim in all the local long distance swim events. The thing that I realized with my pursuit of swimming is that you don't have to be the fastest or the best, you just need to be consistent with your training and make sure your diet supports your endeavors. I gleaned all of this information from listening and watching my Uncle Jack.

I truly enjoyed listening to Jack talk about his time visiting Hawaii and prone paddle boarding with Olympic swimmer and surfing icon, Duke Kahanamoku. Those stories also inspired me to begin a stint of many years of prone and stand-up paddle boarding. I was not a champion, but with Jack's advice to "just get out there and do it", I did it!

Jack's legacy to the world is that everyone who knows of Jack LaLanne or has heard of him is affected by his guidance and behaviour as far as nutrition and physical fitness goes. People paid attention to him!

Three words to describe Jack: he's a BADASS!

Aloha,

Susan LaLanne
Owner, Polynesian Paddling Products, Niece of Jack LaLanne

Chris LaLanne Growing up, I had people ask me, "Are you related to Jack LaLanne?" And I would say, "Yes, I'm Jack's Grandnephew." But, it didn't mean that much to me because I was an adolescent. It didn't have an impact on me until I was 17 years old and I graduated high school. I went to junior college and started to find direction and motivation from my family ties with Jack and the LaLanne legacy. I started to enroll in courses in nutrition, fitness training courses, and that is where people in that field wanted to know more about my connection with the LaLanne's. I realized I had an opportunity to follow in his footsteps and it really allowed me to discover a deeper "why" for me and why it's important for me to pursue this as a career.

Having the LaLanne name is a blessing and responsibility. Everyone I meet, and I ask, they tell me a story about Jack. That's his legacy--the story that is inside every person that he impacted with his message through the television. Generally, it's a story about how he inspired them. Jack was not a personal trainer or fitness instructor. He was your life coach. He talked about exercise and he talked about what to eat and he also talked about taking pride in yourself and having the discipline to show up every day and be a better person by way of making yourself a priority.

Pride, Discipline, and Connection.

When you go back on Youtube and watch the old black and white videos, Jack was talking to YOU, and you felt it. He was looking at YOU. He was telling YOU that he cared about you and he wanted you to care about yourself.

Chris LaLanne
Grand nephew of Jack LaLanne, personal trainer, and owner of LaLanne Bootcamp

Family photo during Face-a-Tonics exercise video. Son Dan produced the video. Circa 1985.

Left to right, Jon Allen, Yvonne and Dan

Jon Allen and wife, Lora

Yvonne and husband, Mark Rubenstein

The LaLanne Bunch: (from left) Jennie (Jack's mother), Hattie, Janet, Yvonne, Jack, Happy, Jon, Elaine, Danny Circa: 1965

Our loving daughter, Janet, passed away in 1973, at age 21, in an automobile accident. Her smile lit up the room. She forever remains in our hearts and memories.

JACK LALANNE

SECTION SEVEN

Fond Memories, Impact, Legacy, and Words that Describe Jack by Some of Those He Inspired

"It's not what you do SOME of the time that counts, it's what you do MOST of the time that counts." – LaLanne-ism

At the end of our lives, when we can turn around and see the ripple effect of our actions on the lives of others, will we be surprised? The countless people whose perspectives we shifted into hope by spending that little bit of extra time showing them how to achieve something we thought was so simple, the countless people whose hope escalated when we worked with them, side by side, to help them see, feel, and taste success, the countless people whose successes we recognized and applauded, feeding their passion and determination for more, and the legacies those individuals are creating because we pursued our passion and gave of ourselves. Will you be surprised? There's always one more challenge awaiting us, one more person we can inspire, one more thing we can do.

Even though "Legacy" never entered Jack's mind, he taught us to share and care, to never say 'never', and to reach outside our perceived limitations because we CAN. He taught us so much more than how to grow a strong and healthy body. All he ever said was, "I want to help people to help themselves." He saw that if only they would help themselves they could change their lives for the better. He believed in simplicity.

Thank you, Jack, for leaving a legacy of possibility, inspiration, and achievement while being an example that we may follow in building and leaving our own legacies.

From Presidents to celebrities, fitness professionals to everyday people, Jack LaLanne inspired tens of millions with his message of exercise, nutrition, positivity and inclusivity. In this section, you'll read amazing stories of inspiration and motivation.

Greg Justice

We conducted countless interviews with now famous names in the modern-day fitness industry and all walks of life. Each of them shared stories about how Jack impacted their careers and lives in general.

Kenneth H. Cooper, MD, MPH I am pleased to be able to make some comments about my long-term friend and colleague, Jack LaLanne.

Even before publishing *Aerobics* in 1968, I had watched Jack's television program on many occasions. I always appreciate his enthusiasm and the example of the phenomenal things he was able to accomplish about how he conditioned and trained himself. To say he was an icon is an understatement. Many people throughout the world followed and participated in Jack's program on television and benefited from it.

I had the opportunity to visit with Jack on many occasions and one time had him come to one of our banquets and be our featured speaker. I distinctly recall how he demonstrated vividly what most people eat for breakfast. And anyone who ever saw one of his programs knows exactly what I am talking about.

Millie and I have both enjoyed our relationship not only with Jack but with Elaine and since Jack has passed away, it has been delightful to exchange Christmas cards every year. As Elaine said, she and Millie are "two peas in a pod" which is an understatement.

I am honored to be asked to contribute some of my comments about this "icon" and do miss the infrequent communications and chances to visit with him. He certainly was a role model for any of us involved in trying to improve the health and fitness of people throughout the world!"

Kenneth H. Cooper, **MD, MPH**
Founder and Chairman, The Cooper Institute, author of bestselling book, "Aerobics."

Favorite Memories From Those He Inspired

Arnold Schwarzenegger I came to America in 1968, and Jack was one of the first people I met at Venice beach. He was very friendly and said, "Come on. Let's work out together, it's so much fun." Boy did I regret that. After 30 minutes of doing chin ups, pushups, dips and leg raises, I was so pumped up that I couldn't move anymore. Then he said, "Let's keep going, isn't this fun?" He kept going for another hour and never stopped. That's when I said to Franco Columbo, "This guy is a machine." Little did I know that one day I would play a machine myself, but Jack was the real machine.

Arnold Schwarzenegger
Olympic Bodybuilder, Actor, Former California Governor of California

Keith Morrison I was assigned to do a story about Jack LaLanne. I had seen his videos as a kid and I was curious to see what he would be like after all those years. I could not have prepared myself for how remarkable this fellow was, and what an amazing time I would have. It left an indelible impression upon me, which has not diminished.

He was so enthusiastic about his message. A lot of people are like that with their messages, but Jack had a special ability to just kind of lift it, and make you feel inspired by spending time with him. That was the essence of that first day. I remember getting swatted on the stomach a few times, and having some trouble doing the pull-ups that he was trying to make me do, but he wasn't so concerned about that. The other eye opener for me was that this wasn't just about becoming a bodybuilder, or some kind of unattainable exercise regime. By that time he had morphed into someone who was tremendously interested in geriatric issues, and how older people could remain vibrant and healthy and vital, until the end of their lives. And, he told me stories about people in their nineties who had these transformations. That, and the enduring emphasis on nutrition, and the right kinds of foods to eat and not to eat. The expression that stayed with me from the very first day is one of his LaLanneisms, as Elaine called them, "If man made it, spit it out," and "Would you give a coffee and cigarette to your dog? No. You'd kill the dog."

Jack had **absolute determination**. He was **committed** to and **enthusiastic** about his message, and he was **inclusive,** because he was the first person to introduce weight training to women and disabled athletes. It wasn't just about bodybuilding, it was spreading the gospel of fitness to everyone. Jack had a special ability to just kind of lift it, and make you feel inspired by spending time with him.

He had a welcoming behavior, which was greater than almost anybody else I've met. I went to his 90th birthday party in New York, and we did a quick story at the same time. It was a moment, not so much that it was remarkable that this 90 year old was still dancing with Elaine and having a wonderful time, but when anyone got a chance to be with him, it was like he was my very best friend in the world was there to greet me. It always felt that way. It was like you were the most important person he had ever met, and he was so glad to see you.

Keith Morrison
Dateline NBC Correspondent

Gilad Janklowic In 1981, when I first got to Hawaii, some friends and I talked about starting a local fitness show. One of the ideas we came up with was to go to Los Angeles and apply to be on *The Jack LaLanne Show*. I had a decent reputation as a fitness instructor in Los Angeles and in Hawaii, and getting exposure on Jack's show would be beneficial. We contacted *The Jack LaLanne Show* and they actually said, "Yes, please come by and we will have you as a guest." When I arrived, Jack met me in person, and I did a segment on his show. One of the things I still remember is him telling me, "Listen, young man, you're going to have your own show someday." Several years later I had my own fitness show on ESPN. When I was turning 40 and Jack was turning 80, I thought it would be a great idea to have him come to Hawaii and be on my show. Elaine and Jack flew to Hawaii and shot five shows with me. From that point on, there was a friendship that continued to develop over the years. His personal story is **inspiring** in how

he developed from a sick child into a bodybuilder, his commitment to fitness throughout his whole life, and the millions of people he impacted. Jack had an **authentic**, genuine desire to help people. He made himself **available.** Anybody and everybody could come up to him no matter the circumstance, and talk to him about health and fitness and he was always available.

Gilad Janklowic
Creator of ESPN TV fitness show 'Bodies in Motion',
'Basic Training the Workout' and 'Total Body Sculpt with Gilad'

Gunnar Peterson I had known about Jack for many years, but the first time I met him in person was at his 90th birthday party. Several years before that, Jack had done a guest appearance on *The Bonnie Hunt Show*. My best friend Mark Derwin, a series regular on the show, had Jack sign my weight lifting belt. He actually personalized it and wrote some very powerful words on it. It is framed and hangs over the office door in my gym. Some people say that having it personalized devalues it. I disagree. To me, that's where the REAL value is.

Gunnar Peterson
Former Los Angeles Lakers' Director of Strength and Endurance. He has worked with athletes from the NBA, NHL, NFL, MLB, USTA, professional boxing (male AND female) and various NCAA sports. Beverly Hills-based trainer to the stars

Lynn C. Allison I spoke to Jack LaLanne many times over several decades. Every time we talked, his genuine love of fitness, his humor and his dedication came through loud and clear. It is a cliché to say that Jack 'walked the talk,' but he truly lived and breathed with passion for physical perfection.

He would do his workout every single morning for two hours, challenging anyone— including me—to go head-to-head with him. Even though Jack was a couple of decades older than me, his workout was way out of my league! Today's generation, for the most part, simply does not have the drive and discipline that Jack was famous for.

The most important memory I have of Jack is his kindness and concern. He was a very funny man, and would light up the phone line with his banter. Jack always remembered who you were, and asked about your health. I cherished the amazing Christmas cards I received from the LaLanne household every single year. The beautiful part of Jack's legacy is that these memories are still alive and well, through his videos, books, famous sayings, and of course his wonderful wife who continues to spread his, and their, word and work.

Lynn C. Allison
Medical Reporter, Author

Doug Briggs Friday, October 5, 2001, a warm and beautiful evening in El Paso, Texas, four of my Olympic weightlifting friends and I were dining outside. I saw Mr. LaLanne exiting the restaurant and said, "Hey, Mr. LaLanne!" He stopped, looked around and proceeded to walk toward our table. He said, "My, you are five good looking, in-shape guys!" as he shook our hands with enough strength to break our hands. He then proceeded to look at our food, analyzing everything we had with a "Good, good, good, bad!" We talked for 15 minutes, and he invited us to his presentation the next day at the Civic Center. When I got home, I called my mom to tell her about my experience and invited her to attend the presentation with me. We drove from Las Cruces, New Mexico and were fortunate enough to get pictures with Mr. LaLanne before the presentation began.

My mom, Josephine Briggs lived to be 98 years old by following Jack LaLanne and his teachings her whole life including juicing.

Mr. LaLanne's influence on me is the reason that I chose to pursue a Ph.D. in Physical Education. My goal is to live to be 100 years old, but only if my quality of life is there and following Jack LaLanne's guidance, I'm sure I'll make it!

Doug Briggs, **Ph.D. Physical Education**
Director of Human Performance for the US ARMY at Fort Bliss

Mark Rothstein I remember watching my grandparents exercise along with *The Jack LaLanne Show*. I had the honor of meeting Jack at The Club Industry Fitness Convention in 1986. I was walking to the elevator with Jack and his wife, Elaine. When we arrived at the elevator, he went to press the button, but not with his finger. He kicked it with his foot. He had amazing flexibility and balance, and he was in his 70's at the time. That was such a great first meeting and memory of my all-time number one mentor.

Mark Rothstein
Two Guinness World Records for endurance rope jumping,
National Fitness Hall of Fame, presenter, and speaker

> **Jack on Flexibility:** When working out I make sure I go to complete extension and contraction. Everytime you flex your muscles they contract and they get better. Muscles have the ability to contract and extend and when pushed to complete extension and contraction, they become stronger, firmer and more flexible.

Sharron Moran I was a member of the golf team while attending the University of Arizona. During a trip to Palm Springs, where I was working with my golf coach, Al King, he asked me if I would like to play golf the next day with Jack and Elaine LaLanne. Being from a small town in Illinois, I had never been exposed to Jack's fitness shows or his reputation. We teed it up the next morning and had a pleasant round of golf. Both of them had excellent golf games. It was easy to see how much this couple was interested in good health. We talked about everything ranging from finger-tip push ups to improved nutrition. While Elaine and I had lunch while Jack went to the driving range. After lunch we headed back to the course for another eighteen holes. I expressed needing a break, and heard Jack, after looking at his watch, say, "Great, I have time to get to the gym and do my workout." Here they were almost twice my age and full of energy. Jack and Elaine were very encouraging and answered my questions about fitness. They even sent me books and stretch straps (called the Glamour Stretcher) to help build up my strength.

They have been a blessing in my life for more than 59 years, and I am very thankful. We miss Jack, but Elaine, at 96, is doing great and she is definitely still moving at a zippy pace.

Sharron Moran
Golf Pro Rookie of the Year 1967

Kathy Smith Jake Steinfeld had organized a group that included Richard Simmons, Tamilee Webb and Jack LaLanne and me. We met to discuss a concept restaurant that would serve nutritious food. This is where I got a better understanding of Jack's values and how he was driven. He had a set of core beliefs that he stuck to. When anyone would suggest serving things like burgers, or fries, Jack would literally stand up and say, "I am not going to entertain the notion that I would actually be involved with something that wasn't in complete alignment with everything I preach and everything I live." I remember him saying, "You can have excuses or you can have results, but you can't have both." He **empowered** people to be the finest and best they could be. He was driven and had a **big heart**. Jack would give you his energy and his time. When you gave to him, he gave in return. He was a **visionary**--whether it was opening the first modern day health spa, inventing fitness equipment or having the first TV exercise show. He was creating until the day he took his last breath.

Kathy Smith
Fitness Entrepeneur, podcaster, host of Alive and Well TV show

Tamilee Webb There was a big fitness event in San Francisco. I remember getting on stage and Jack standing there. I thought, "Oh my God, I've made it. I'm sharing a stage with Jack LaLanne, the Father of Fitness." It was breathtaking because I grew up watching him and never imagined meeting him. I was a little nervous, and he calmed me. He was like my father. He told me how it's done. He got up there [on stage] and made everybody feel comfortable. This was before I developed the Buns of Steel program.

The funniest story I have of Jack was when Richard Simmons, Jack, Jake Steinfeld (Body by Jake), Kathy Smith, Elaine, and myself, (pictured above) were talking about possibly putting together a restaurant called Planet Fitness. We thought, "Wow, maybe this is a way to bring healthy foods to people." Back then we were told people are not going to buy healthy food. We had all met in LA, and when you get us five together, there's always going to be someone who wants to stand out; that was Richard and Jack. Richard and Jack were always clowning around. I remember Jake saying, "Okay, it's time for us to start this meeting. Let's all sit in our chairs, and have this meeting." I look over and Jack is doing full-on tricep dips with his legs straight out. Due to everyone's other business commitments, the restaurant idea never took off, but it was a lot of fun getting together with your peers and people that you respect and admire.

Tamilee Webb
Hall of Fame Fitness Instructor and creator of "Buns of Steel" fitness program series

Jake Steinfeld Jack LaLanne is a pioneer of fitness, he was the first person to bring fitness to the masses, that's his legacy. I got to know Jack well during our days at HSN. He was authentic. People trusted him. That's something you can't buy. He lived the "Jack LaLanne" lifestyle 24 hours a day, seven days a week. He talked the talk and walked the walk. When I think of Jack LaLanne, I envision hope, health, and family. He gave people hope through his words of encouragement. He gave people the gift of health through his workouts and nutrition guidance. Family was everything to Jack. He loved his family and wanted the best for them. There will never be another Jack LaLanne, he is "The Godfather of Fitness."

Jake Steinfeld
American actor, fitness personality, entrepreneur and producer, developer of "Body by Jake" brand.

Doug Brolus Like most people, I first saw Jack on my grandmother's TV at a young age. At 15, I called the studio in California and asked to speak with Jack. The man on the phone said he was doing his show and he took my number. The phone rang a little later and it was Jack! I was in shock. At 23 years old, Jack invited me to his house in the Hollywood Hills. He showed me his personal gym complete with weights and other  equipment he invented. He gave me the greatest tips on exercise. One such tip was to train with heavy weight, do five to eight reps per set to build up the fast twitch fibers for growth. After a couple of weeks, change over to 15 to 20 reps per set and this will give you great endurance. I would call Jack every two weeks and talk about training and nutrition. Jack and his wife Elaine are the kindest people I have ever met and I think the world of both of them. Jack changed my life with all his fantastic training tips.

Doug Brolus
Bodybuilder and fan

Dr. Fabrizio Mancini As president of Parker University of Chiropractic, I was honored to host Jack's 94th birthday party when he came to Dallas for an event. We filled up the auditorium with 5000 people. I had the Dallas Mavericks cheerleaders bring out a cake for him on stage. What was really interesting happened before that, I was able to take him to NBC to do an interview. Since he was in town, the local affiliate wanted to share what it's like to turn 94 years old and share his words of wisdom. Walking into the studio, they were prepping for him. The host was sitting down and getting mic'd and Jack was asked by the producer to sit down and get mic'd, too. Jack was walking very slow, like if he was a hundred years old. I could see the announcer's face, like, "Oh my God, he's really old." As soon as the interview began, she asked him a question and he just all of a sudden transformed from his crippled position and energetically said, "I'm glad you asked me that."

It blew her away. I can only imagine the hundreds of thousands of people watching the news that day. He wanted to show the typical image of a 94 year old in the United States and around the world as somebody who doesn't have any energy, who is all wrinkled, with no vibrancy. When he came into his being, whether it was on the show, or on the stage later that day, he made us, in our 20's and 30's, feel like we were just getting started.

I will always thank Jack for that moment in Dallas. Living by the principles he taught, I feel like I'm getting younger and younger everyday.

Dr. Fabrizio Mancini
Internationally acclaimed chiropractor, bilingual speaker, author,
educator, philanthropist; and former president of Parker University

Kathie & Peter Davis My very first memory of Jack was when I was a little girl, about 6 years old. I saw him on TV because my mom used to work out with him. She would hold onto the chair and do squats and leg lifts. I remember being mesmerized by my mom doing all these exercises. Fast forward to when Peter and I presented him with the IDEA Lifetime Achievement Award, to my surprise, he picked me up on the stage and lifted me high up in the air. I was shocked that this man could even lift me up!

Kathie & Peter Davis
Founders of IDEA Health & Fitness Association

Gary Player *A message sent to Elaine LaLanne on her 90th birthday.*

Jack would be very, very proud of you. He loved you so much. I really miss him. What always amazes me (is) that all these athletes, with all their athletic prowess, get recognition from the President of America and yet when Jack died, he did more than any of them, saving tens of millions of lives (and) was never acknowledged to the extent that (he) should be.

Gary Player
Golf Professional The Black Knight

Francene Green-Litteral In 1983 I had just sold my Pepperidge Farm franchise and was eager to move on to my next adventure with Celebrity Foods, which held the license for Jack LaLanne Bread and related products. I was given the assignment of finding a reputable bakery that would bake his breads and accept the ingredients Jack approved. In 1983 and 1984, most breads contained unbleached flour and

good nutrition wasn't foremost in most people's minds. Very few bakeries were up to the challenge. Jack never deviated from his beliefs and it was evident that money was no object; it was his desire that the ingredients be beneficial to the consumer's health. After the ingredients, came the packaging. When they called me to come and "push the button" for the first roll out of the bread wrapper, I can't explain the feeling that came

over me when the first bags came rolling by me on the conveyor belt. It was one of the most extraordinary moments in time that I will never forget.

Francene Green-Litteral
Former Pepperidge Farm franchise owner
Designer of Jack LaLanne Bread and Cereal products

John Cates I have a Jack LaLanne hat that I wear everywhere. So many people notice my hat and tell me stories about watching Jack on TV. In fact, the first time I saw Jack LaLanne was on TV in 1952. I remember telling my mom, "I want to be like him!" From that moment on, he dictated my life.

The press showed up in droves in 1994 when Jack was given The State of California Governor's Council on Physical Fitness Lifetime Achievement Award. It was Jack's 80th birthday, and it reintroduced Jack to an entirely new generation. There were more than 100 state leaders at this event and Jack asked each one, "Have you worked out today?" It was also Jack's wedding anniversary, and I remember him singing, "If You Were the Only Girl in the World" to his wife, Elaine (Lala).

There was another time, while visiting the LaLanne home, we were sitting around the kitchen while Lala was cooking. Jack was encouraging me, when he said, "Listen, John. I've done a lot of things, but so have you. I want to impact people. I enjoy people. I enjoy encouraging everyone to stay in shape. It's all about lifestyle." Jack was humble, enthusiastic and positive. There will never be another Jack.

John Cates
Former Executive Director of the President's Council on Physical Fitness and Sports,
Former Executive Director of California Governor's Council on Physical Fitness and Sports

Cory Everson The first time I ever heard the name Jack LaLanne was in 1979. University of Wisconsin strength coach, Jeff Everson, explained to the women's track & field athletes that in order to be successful in our individual events, we needed to develop something he called "functional muscle." This was the type of muscle that combined power and strength with endurance, and the type of muscle preached by one of Jeff's mentors, Jack LaLanne. As a college athlete, this became my goal.

I still remember Jeff telling our track and field team this insane story about 70 year old Jack swimming across the Long Beach Harbor while towing 70 people in 70 boats while shackled and handcuffed. It all seemed so far-fetched until I saw the photographs of Jack in an old "Strength and Health" magazine. Jack's physique resembled the well-toned bodies of our best gymnasts and pole vaulters. Through Jeff, I had visions of Jack flexing in my head way before I ever thought about competing in bodybuilding.

We were blessed to meet Jack and Elaine at various functions throughout the United States--from Olympia competitions to supershow events. Together they drew more fans than the Chicago Bulls. People waited patiently in lines to take a personal photo with the first couple of fitness. When the Grand Princess took its inaugural voyage, we were invited along with Lee Haney, Davy Jones (the Monkees), Bob Keeshan, (Captain Kangaroo), Jack and Elaine and many others.

In 1985, Jack's show ended and shortly thereafter we produced our fitness show on ESPN, and then later another on ESPN2. Needless to say, *The Jack LaLanne Show* paved the way for so many fitness shows to be aired on TV, bringing more achievable health into the home.

In 2012, Jack (posthumously) and I, along with Randy Couture, and strongman Mark Henry, were awarded the Schwarzenegger International Sports Hall of Fame Achievement Award. This award was accepted by Elaine and this is where our friendship continued to grow, and we became fast friends. Not only is Jack a role model but Elaine has become my role model as well. I have never met a more loving, positive, sparkling woman. For close to a century the LaLanne lifestyle has sculpted our lives encouraging better mind, body, spirit, and health. I am eternally grateful for this dynamic duo.

Cory Everson
American body building champion, actress

Robert Blackstone I was doing research at Harvard Graduate School of Education when I was diagnosed with stage four lymphoma. I had a lump on the side of my neck about the size of a grape. Turns out there were so many more tumors all over my body that they wanted to do emergency surgery the next day. My survival rate was about 20%. So I started chemotherapy.

The feeling of chemo is like the flu. Being a smaller guy, I lost weight quickly. I was advised to take a class about facing the final stages of life. The weight of having to make those decisions was more than any weight I ever touched at the gym. At some point during this process I started to fight. I changed my nutrition. My workouts started again with two bodybuilders who thought I might be shaving my hair to look like Mr. Clean. I never told them I was sick. They pushed me hard.

Cancer allowed me access to Harvard and MIT professors to talk about their research on nutrition or bone and muscle loss. I talked to my surgeon about the effect of weight training on my picc line. My surgeon who had been placing picc lines since the Vietnam war could not determine if bench pressing a lot of weight might be harmful. He said no one had ever asked him that when they had cancer. There were more questions than answers.

I had been hearing about juicing and was curious about it. It was determined a juicing regimen might be beneficial, but no one knew which vegetables or how much. One of my friends called Jack LaLanne to see if he would talk to me. He said yes.

Jack spoke to me at length. He was compassionate, funny and very real. After telling him my story, I asked him if juicing would help me. He softened his voice and got serious. He did not give some off the cuff answer, instead he said, "Robert, remember this, no one can tell you the right amount of anything. When it really counts, you need to figure it out yourself." There is no cookie- cutter formula. It was the most honest and heartfelt answer that anyone gave me. That insight told me a lot about how he became so successful and helped so many. No one told him how many reps to do or how to do great things. Jack studied and told himself and reminded the world that "anything was possible if you believe."

I started to research nutrition plans and superfoods. I increased my vitamins and food intake toward more protein and vegetables and increased my workouts. I became stronger. At one point I recouped my normal weight and even added 20 pounds of muscle. I was in better shape at the end of six months of chemotherapy than a year before. The difference came from the food I ate, hard training and a strong belief in what was possible.

I was inspired by Jack's great balancing acts and many pushups which lead to me doing one-handed push ups with only three fingers to show my determination. I would later set a company record in Army boot camp by doing 121 push ups in 120 seconds. I had friends that would become bodybuilders as I became a Black Belt.

Being Apache Indian (Native American) we have tremendous respect for our ancestors. During sweat lodges, similar to a sauna, we bring in hot stones, called "grandfathers," that heat the water up to almost 180 degrees to push our limits. Jack was a hot stone of a grandfather pushing us all. I can hear him say, maybe even sing, "Anything is possible if you just believe." He helped save my life and gave me some clear meaning and purpose.

Robert Blackstone
Chairman for the Educational Board
for the National Association of Sports Medicine (NASM)

Rich Benyo My brother, Drew, and I tried many times to make a gym out of our living room and dining room furniture. We were trying to do what Jack said we needed to do: turn our scrawny little kid bodies into an anatomical "V" just like Jack's broad shoulders and slim waist. Our father wasn't keen on this, so my brother and I begrudgingly returned the chairs to their rightful places. In our attempt at being Charles Atlas, we realized Jack was better than Charles Atlas because we could watch him on the old concrete-block TV that squatted in our living room.

Years later I would get to meet Jack while I collaborated with his wife Elaine (LaLa) on five fitness-oriented books. Although physically Jack wasn't anywhere as massive as I had pictured him as a child, he was a massive presence. The Jack we met at his house in

Morro Bay was the Jack who was on the television show--full of energy, smiling, pumped, ready to reach out and nudge you along on the road to wellness.

That had been Jack's allure on television. He came across as a guy with both a mission and a sense of humor about life and the world in general. He didn't take himself very seriously while still being very serious about his mission to make America, and the world, healthier and happier.

His dedication to routine was legendary. Every morning, when my wife Rhonda (also a childhood fan) and I we were guests of the LaLanne's, we could tell when it was 4:00 a.m. because we could hear Jack clanging the weights in his home gym, then he would move to the pool for another hour.

In everything he did, he strove to share both his enthusiasm and what he had learned, hoping to enhance the lives of people around him. He stressed that nobody and nothing is perfect, and if we get hung up on the concept of perfect, we are going to defeat ourselves. As Jack often said, "It's not what you do some of the time that counts, it's what you do most of the time that counts." Sounds like a philosophy anyone who strives for a better life can live with. Thanks for sharing, Jack.

Rich Benyo
Editor, Marathon & Beyond Magazine,
journalist, author, former editor of Runner's World Magazine

Frank "Poncho" Sampedro At age 16, I moved from Detroit out to LA on my own and enrolled myself in Hollywood High School.

There I got to know Danny. Through him, I met Jack and Elaine LaLanne, his sisters Janet and Yvonne, Hattie, the housekeeper, and Jon Allen, who was two or three at the time. I felt very comfortable at the LaLanne house which was full of smiles, welcomes, and lots of love; such a positive place for a 16 year old who was mostly broke and hungry.

Elaine always stuck out in my mind because she treated me with such kindness and respect. She had an honest belief in me, which was part of the whole LaLanne aura. Jack's positivity was everywhere and his big smile, along with a pat on the back, made me feel like I was doing good just being in the house.

The first time I went into Jack's gym, I was taken aback! There were so many chrome dumbbells all lined up in racks along with machines, benches and mirrors everywhere. It was like a Disneyland workout.

I went over to his squat rack and put my shoulders under the bar that was holding 250 pounds. Danny started laughing and said, "Don't hurt yourself." I got the bar off of the rack and did a half a squat, and felt lucky to get it back on the rack. Danny told me that none of his friends could ever even move it. I felt so proud inside! I felt Jack's enthusiasm, his drive, and his energy.

Getting to spend the night at the house was a real bonus for me! I'll never forget hearing splashing very early one morning. I looked out the window and in the pool was Jack with a cord strapped to a belt around his waist, that only allowed him to get three-fourths of the way across the pool and swimming like Jaws was chasing him! I would be back to sleep before he stopped!

One of the things that sticks out in my mind was a framed letter in Jack's trophy case. It was from the warden at Alcatraz asking Jack to please not swim from Fisherman's Wharf to the Island any more because it encouraged the prisoners to try and escape. Danny and I would often be sitting on the couch making 8-track tapes, and Jack would come in and see us just sitting there. Soon, we would be listening to another lecture about how sitting on the couch gets you nowhere in life! (Stand up, get moving, inspire yourself and that will help inspire others!) Then on his way out he would say, "Hey, you guys brush Happy, OK?" We would start brushing but as soon as Jack left the room Happy would growl at us. We got the message.

Danny worked in the shipping department at LaLanne, Inc. and after we graduated from Hollywood High, he was going off to a semester at sea college and invited me to take his place at his job. While working for Jack, I learned so much about fitness, food, and the importance of vitamins. We would mail exercise booklets and cookbooks. To this day I still eat meals from that book and use the cooking tips, too.

When I learned that Jack could do 1,000 push ups and 1,000 chin ups, I was ready to try. I never got there, but my best was 1,000 sit ups and I did them every day for 30 years. I always remember Jack's words, "You have to be able to help yourself so you can pass it on." I still think of those words, and at 72, I swim in the ocean every day and try as hard as I can to keep a streak going. One of the main things he taught me was that endurance training was so much more important than lifting heavy weights.

Jack touched many people and came up with many workout and health innovations! He was amazing and unselfish.

Frank "Poncho" Sampedro
Crazy Horse – Rhythm guitarist for Neil Young

Lee Flaherty *Here are a couple of excerpts from a 2010 speech by Lee Flaherty, a close friend of Jack, and founder of Flair Communications and fellow member of the Horatio Alger Association when he received a Legendary Landmark Honor in Chicago. Lee is now in his 80's and continues to tell stories about how Jack LaLanne inspired him.*

In the mid-1950's I met Jack LaLanne while he was a human tugboat. He was pulling a boat that weighed more than 1-ton in the San Francisco Bay. In 1977, when I founded the Mayor's Marathon/Chicago I told him I was discouraged about not finding sponsors as no one believed in it. Jack told me about his early days when his ideas were ridiculed but he wouldn't give up and held on to become famous with his TV show on health and fitness. Jack convinced me to persevere. I did, and now Chicago's Marathon is the world's largest with 45,000 runners, generates $343 million in city revenue, and annually raises $421 million for over 100 charities. Without Jack's (and my mother's inspiration), I might not have been able to make a success of my life.

Lee Flaherty
Founder of Flair Communications, fellow member of Horatio Alger Association

Todd Smith Jack indirectly introduced my father and mother, which led our family into the fitness industry. My brother, Chad and I, as well as my brother-in-law Bret, are still in the health club business in Las Vegas. My mother met Elaine in the early 1940's in Minnesota when she and Elaine were both part of a synchronized swimming team that performed annually in the Minneapolis Aqua Follies. Both Elaine and my mother were athletic and enjoyed entertaining, and they both moved to the west coast to pursue their careers.

My father, Rudy Smith, first met Jack at Muscle Beach in Southern California, a short distance away from Culver City where he grew up. He was in his late teens and was watching Jack and his buddies perform on the rings, acrobatics/gymnastics, human pyramids and feats of strength. My father asked Jack how he developed his phenomenal muscle mass, assuming that it didn't come from their activities at Muscle Beach, and Jack told him "you have to lift weights."

My father joined a gym, started weight lifting, and years later was hired by Vic Tanny, rose to the rank of VP of Sales, and was Vic Tanny's right hand man. After a short stint in acting at the Pasadena Playhouse in Southern California, my mother also went to work for Vic Tanny's Gyms. She eventually became the women's manager at the San Francisco gym on Market Street. When the men's manager was out sick, my father went up to San

Francisco to substitute for him. This was about when my parents started dating. Elaine, unbeknownst to my mother, was working at KGO-TV as a television show producer and on air personality. Elaine and Jack had also started dating. Then on one of my parent's dates, Jack and Elaine ran into them at a restaurant. Elaine excitedly bellowed, "Ginny, what are you doing here?" (Elaine was the one that told me that part of the story, and she remembered the name of the restaurant too--Original Joe's.) They stayed friends throughout the years. Jack even sang Happy Birthday to my father at his 60th birthday party, as well as my parent's joint 80th birthday party and 50th anniversary celebrations.

Todd Smith
CEO of Las Vegas Athletic Clubs and son of Rudy Smith

Jan Todd In the history of fitness there have been many celebrities but only a few icons. What's the difference? Celebrities are people who are famous—who are in the public's eye for a period of time, they attract some publicity—but then they fade from the public's gaze. Most winners of the Mr. Olympia contest, for example, are/were celebrities. However, of those champions, Arnold Schwarzenegger will always be remembered by future historians as an icon.

Fitness icons transcend mere celebrity; they are people who change the world of fitness. Icons are the athletes who push the boundaries of what was previously thought possible in terms of strength, endurance, muscularity or creating a beautiful physique. They are also innovators and inventors who revolutionize the world of fitness-- like Dr. Kenneth Cooper did when he introduced the concept of aerobics--and then jogging and aerobic dance sprang up around the globe.

Jack LaLanne is an icon. He didn't start his career in fitness with that intention. His life and contributions go far beyond celebrity. LaLanne's physique, his promotion of healthy eating, his public exhibitions of his own fitness, and his endless enthusiasm and energy, made him unique in the world of television and fitness. There was no one like him.

As is the case for so many others, Jack LaLanne was my first introduction to the world of fitness. I also watched his program when I was a girl along with my mother and sister, and listened to what he had to say.

He's an icon because before we even knew there was a "world of fitness," Jack was already changing the paradigm and normalizing the practice of exercise and healthy eating for us all. He was the true game changer. And that's why, at the H.J. Lutcher Stark Center, at the

University of Texas, Terry and I made sure that Jack LaLanne's photo hangs prominently on our Wall of Icons in Physical Culture.

Director and Professor,
H.J. Lutcher Stark Center at University of Texas

Rick Hersh I've represented Jack and Elaine for 40 years, most of the time with the William Morris Agency. I have represented numerous celebrities but Jack was the most original and there will never be anyone else quite like him.

Jack dedicated his life to 4 things: fitness, health, how to live a healthy life, and his wife Elaine. He had tremendous discipline, dedication, focus, determination and energy.

He loved trying to help the average American improve their fitness which is why *The Jack LaLanne Show* remained on the air for 34 years; at the time, a Guinness World Record for a fitness show.

Jack was a great athlete that included being a world class bodybuilder, pioneer fitness innovator, motivator, swimmer, and a near scratch golfer; often playing with his good friend Gary Player. Jack had a gift for being part fitness evangelist, promoter, entertainer, a great communicator, very funny, quick witted, and did I mention he loved to sing.

Jack and Elaine were also creators and inventors having written numerous books, created the first Instant Breakfast and rubber stretchers, and much of the equipment concepts you currently see in gyms today. However, back in that day, he was so busy that he never bothered with patents and trademarks so others ended up creating new innovations.

He began juicing at an early age and later in life came out with the Jack LaLanne Juicer which sold millions. He also was known for his catchy one liners such as "If man made it don't eat it", "I can't die; it would wreck my image", "I don't love exercising but I love the results." Jack was the originator of modern fitness and he was so far ahead of the world that all of his principals hold up well even today.

Jack LaLanne IS The Godfather of Health and Fitness!

Rick Hersh
President, Celebrity Consultants,
Former Vice President of William Morris Agency

Judi Sheppard Missett We were at a governor's council meeting at Lake Tahoe, which went great. I had a big stretch limo ready to take me to the airport, and Elaine and Jack, who were also flying out of Reno, were standing outside the hotel.

150   JACK LALANNE

Judi and Jack at the Great California
Workout circa 1990s.

I asked, "Why don't you come along." They jumped right in!

I loved that it was just the 4 of us! My friend Shanna was with me. Jack was gracious and funny. We also discovered that Elaine was just as energetic as Jack. She was bubbly and kind and delightful. Jack spent the hour-long car ride telling us funny stories, but you could tell he didn't feel like he had to be performing for anybody. It was a very human side of him, which I loved. As a performer myself, it was great to see him let his guard down and just be Jack.

Judi Sheppard Missett
Founder of Jazzercise

Tony Horton It was the early stages of my career, I was training Bruce Springsteen, Annie Lennox, Tom Petty, Billy Idol, Lindsey Buckingham, Stevie Nicks and Stephen Stills, plus celebrities like Sean Connery, Shirley McClain, Bryce Dallas Howard, Allison Janney, Octavia Spencer, and more.

Before I found my fitness career, I was a C minus student with a speech impediment who lived on sugar cereal and fast food. It was inspiring for me to later learn that Jack ate poorly too, and had a rough time of it as a kid.

I was in the Atlanta airport walking down a terminal to catch a flight, when I practically ran right into Jack and Elaine coming off their plane. The man! The Godfather of Fitness just strolling through the airport. I had followed his career for decades, watching him on television, following his feats of strength, his infomercials. Here was my one chance to say hello and introduce myself.

When I told him that I was a fitness trainer, he couldn't have been more polite, engaging, and enthusiastic. He didn't know me from Adam, but he wanted me to know how important it was that I help as many people as I could. He made fitness training sound like the most important career in the world.

Tony Horton
2016 winner of the Jack LaLanne Award
through Idea World, Creator of P90X program

Stu Shostak Jack and Elaine came into my life while I was barely into my 30's. I was recommended to them as a film archivist to help them organize their video library because at the time I was doing the same for Lucille Ball. I not only became a part-time employee but a lifelong friend. I came to realize very quickly just how much Jack believed every single thing he practiced and preached. I grew up watching Jack do daily exercises every morning on his TV show and it certainly did not stop when the cameras were turned off. Jack's life was truly based on being physically fit by eating the right kinds of foods and exercising - this was and still is the key to a long, healthy life. At nearly 65, and over 33 years since I first met the LaLannes, I've been able to maintain my weight by doing exactly what Jack said to do, and I still feel great. Trust me, what he said and did, WORKS! He was a master at his craft.

Stu Shostak
Host, "Stu's Show", www.stusshow.com

Brooks Wachtel I first saw Jack LaLanne in black and white and a few inches tall on a flickering screen. That was television in the 1950's. Even as a young kid I admired his energy and passion. In the early 60's President Kennedy encouraged the nation to embrace physical fitness – and called Jack to be a founding member of the President's Council on Physical Fitness. So there was Jack doing his patriotic duty on my television screen and, save for a change in my personal geography, that was where the relationship might have stayed. When my folks moved to Los Angeles, I attended Hollywood High School and there I became friends with the LaLanne's daughter, Janet. And, of course, I met Jack. I discovered his television persona was not a persona at all, it was him!

Regretfully, my friend Janet LaLanne passed away at age 21 in an auto accident, yet as the years went on I became closer to the family and did artwork, writing, and voice-overs. When Jack had another television show, I helped find on-camera guests. Jack was a consummate professional and knew show business inside and out. When I started writing Saturday morning animation, Jack surprised me by knowing exactly the amount of the script fees.

He was a lot more than a video work-out trainer, he knew the message he wanted to share and exactly how to use the medium to do it. In person he set an example. If you followed his approach to life, he was there with advice and encouragement. If you didn't, and I did not, it was never an issue at all.

He also knew to surround himself with the best and he found the perfect partner who could guide and organize him through show-business and life, his equally remarkable wife, Elaine. They made a perfect team, a harmonizing duet that counterpointed each impeccably.

Jack was also fun. His engaging energy was always delightful and when spending time with Jack you knew you were in the presence of a unique, kind and amazing person.

Brooks Wachtel
Emmy Award Winning Screenwriter, Producer, Author

Heidi Powell I was aware of Jack at a very young age. My maiden name was Lane. I would hear people talk about Jack LaLanne, and I thought they were talking about my grandpa, Jack Lane. I thought my grandpa was amazing, and I believed that he was the godfather of modern fitness. I couldn't understand why no one could say my Grandpa Jack's last name right. It's Jack Lane, not Jack LaLanne. When I was about eight years old, my parents were watching Jack's program and that's when it clicked. It was Jack LaLanne! Not my grandpa.

Jack and Elaine created the ideal example of family fitness for me and for my parents, who raised us in a way that was in line with all of the things that Jack was teaching the world. My parents were some of the only people who I knew eating protein bars and drinking protein shakes when nobody else was, taking me to the gym with them when I was a teenager. This exposure at a young age led me to become a gymnast, a cheerleader, then a trainer. To this day, I still follow Jack's lead in how I teach people.

I still remember his Alcatraz swim with his hands cuffed and feet shackled, the jumping jacks, a thousand pushups. I love that he did these things as he aged. He defied what the world today still believes--that as we age, we get weaker. He proved the opposite. My favorite stories were about his strength, and his almost superhuman nature.

I have such an appreciation for the way that Jack devoted his life to something much greater than himself. He did not do it for fame or recognition. He did it to prove that it's never too late. Age doesn't matter. He opened our eyes to things that we never would have thought about otherwise. He taught us that anything is possible. It was very much like Walt Disney style. If you can dream it, you can do it. Whether you believe you can or you can't, you're right.

As Jack always advocated in his very famous quote, "Anything is possible, if you make it happen."

Best-selling author, speaker, trainer, transformation specialist.
ABC's Extreme Weight Loss host with Chris Powell.
Awarded the 2018 IDEA Jack LaLanne Award.

Kevin O'Connell I met Jack through my friend, Carl Cathay. Carl worked for Jack and considered him a mentor. Carl opened the Executive Athlete Club in Oakland, California in 1955, and I opened my club in the early 1970's.

Jack was the leader of the band, and he wanted nothing more than to spread the news of health & fitness. I remember saying to him, "Jack you're the real deal," and he would say, "Pass it on." He wanted us to keep passing on the message to anyone that would listen.

Three words that come to mind when I think about Jack LaLanne are **love**, **respect**, and **dedication**. He also had a great sense of humor.

Former gym owner and close friend of Jack

From Elaine: Unfortunately, Kevin O'Connell passed on to the next expression of his life shortly after giving us this quote. He was dedicated to the world of health and fitness and his legacy along with Jack's and all the people in fitness will keep passing it on.

Jaime Brenkus Denise Austin introduced me to Jack as "The 8 Minute Abs guy." He responded by putting me in a headlock and giving me a nuggy and said, "That's what's wrong with you guys. You only think there's one body part?" It was so funny, and had everyone laughing, including Jack. He then said, "No, I'm just kidding, I love you!" At 90 years old, he was so full of energy.

Co-Author with Elaine LaLanne, "If You Want to Live, MOVE.
Putting the Boom back in Bommers" Creator of "8-Minute Abs" video series

What Impact Did Jack LaLanne Have On Your Life?

Not only did Jack inspire so many, he left an impact! Below are the impactful moments that were discussed in recent interviews.

Joe De Sena There is NO JOE without JACK. Jack was the much bigger, badder, stronger and advanced Joe. He inspired my mom. My mom inspired me. And Spartan was born. So Elaine is the MATRIARCH of Spartan.

Joe De Sena
Founder, CEO Spartan Race, author

Keith Morrison The engaging part about Jack is his incredible enthusiasm to have a student around to show what was possible. He was like an evangelist, like a preacher.

Keith Morrison
Dateline NBC Correspondent

Gunnar Peterson Jack LaLanne is definitely a force in my life, not just professionally, but in how I carry myself. He set the table in the fitness industry for all of us. There should be a "Jack LaLanne Day" where every trainer and fitness professional gives thanks to the man who started it all. Jack LaLanne also made us all accountable and responsible for our own health and wellbeing. That has had even more of an impact on me. I'm not a victim of my physical circumstances. I'm in control.

Gunnar Peterson
Former Los Angeles Lakers Director of Strength and Endurance.
Also affiliated with NBA, NHL, NFL, MLB, USTA, professional boxing and NCAA.
Beverly Hills-based trainer to the stars

Dan Isaacson I had developed and opened the first personal training and fitness centers at Paramount Pictures and Sony Pictures Entertainment. I had been around the greatest actors and entertainers in the world. Then I met Jack LaLanne, and Elaine, at a meeting with the California Governor's Council on Physical Fitness and Sports.

Jack loved family, friends, country and approached his calling in life truthfully, **honestly** and with **respect** for all people! The cornerstones to his greatness are reflected through great Americans who also reflect the values of celebrating diversity and inclusivity in America! His legacy of fitness innovation, nutritional education, people friendly programming and his humorous and charismatic leadership is unmatched! He taught people what he knew to be **true**, never looking for credit, and encouraged everyone to get started. He followed his mother's advice to change his unhealthy lifestyle as a boy to a lifestyle of vibrant good health as an adult!

Dan Isaacson
Former director of California Governor's Council on Physical Fitness,
President of Isaacson Fitness, LLC, public speaker

Melissa Johnson Jack was in his 80's when we worked together on the California Governor's Council on Physical Fitness and Sports. He energized everyone at our events with rousing speeches, encouraging words, and fun exercises. He had a lasting impact by how he led by example and genuinely cared about the health and wellness of Californians. One of my favorite memories was him belting out, "Take me out to the ball game" with gusto at the Angels Stadium for our active seniors day. It's a special memory I shared with my parents.

Melissa Johnson
Former Executive Director,
President's Council on Physical Fitness & Sports
and California Governor's Council on Physical Fitness & Sports

Mark Rothstein I founded and produced my first rope jumping instructional video in 1991 and I sent Jack two copies. With the videos, there was a letter asking if he would do me the honor of accepting one as a gift, and sending one back with his autograph, so I could put it in my home fitness museum. Not only did he autograph and send the video back, but he also called my office and said, 'Mark, I want you to know you're doing a hell of a job.' I literally break out in a cold sweat when I think back to that moment. Here I was talking to my all-time mentor, my hero. That phone call was so powerful and inspirational to me.

Mark Rothstein
Two Guinness World Records for endurance rope jumping,
National Fitness Hall of Fame, presenter, and speaker

Kathy Smith In the early '80s, I was doing a television show called *Alive and Well*. I had the privilege of not only doing fitness, but also lifestyle segments. As part of that journey, I was able to go to Jack and Elaine's house in the Hollywood Hills. When I went there, Jack was outside by the pool. So I walked out to the pool to see him tethered to the side doing laps. When he finally popped out, he was beyond belief in shape. He told me that he had spent the last hour doing laps but that was after he had already done an hour and a half in his gym.

I was at the beginning of my fitness career and that was our first meeting. I felt he was a prophet. I looked up to him and hung on every word. I lost my parents when I was a teenager, so my involvement with health and fitness improved my mental outlook. He embodied all the principles that changed my life, pulled me out of a depression and kept me on track. This had a big impact on me.

He was the first person that I ran into who spoke my language; spoke what I felt in my heart. I knew that a healthy lifestyle--eating right, taking care of your body was the foundation for everything else we do.

Kathy Smith
Fitness Entrepeneur, podcaster, host of Alive and Well TV show

Dr. Roger Russo Yes, Jack was the Godfather of Fitness but he also should be known as the Godfather of Motivation. When I met and worked with him I realized that was what Jack was all about. He motivated people and often said, "God helps those who help themselves." He was respected for it because it came from his heart. In my chiropractic office he still motivates my patients while they exercise. One time while shooting a commercial for me, the script called for his show's closing song, the last line being, "may the good Lord bless and keep you." To all of our surprise he added, "and keep up your Chiropractic!" To all that knew him, he was classic Jack, the real deal. He truly was the real deal on or off camera.

Dr. Roger Russo
Chiropractor, Founder Stay Fit Circuit

Bill Crawford I had just opened a Nautilus club in the early 1980s, and we were having our grand opening event. Exercise wasn't fully accepted by the masses. Many in the medical profession were still suspicious of weight resistance exercise. They said it would make you muscle bound and wear out your joints. My friends and family thought I had gone off the deep end. They said, "Bill, you need to get a real job, there's no future in this." Jack walked in and he said, "Kid, fitness is here to stay, and you're on the right track. Stick with it." He was powerful in his presence and electrified the room. He was a **Supreme Couch Evictor**. He would get people off of their couches. He didn't do it by shaming them or scolding them. He did it by his masterful ability to encourage and motivate people. He showed many that there was a pathway to do this as a career, to have a job where you're encouraging and teaching people to exercise. He planted the seeds for an industry that has impacted millions of people around the world. He was really strong on ideals and morals, and those were woven into his exercise programs.

Bill Crawford
Owner of Basic Training in Arizona, former owner of
Nautilus fitness centers in Los Angeles with Arthur Jones

Peter Twist I was impacted by Jack even before I met him in person. Looking back I remember thinking, who is this passionate, crazy guy advocating and talking about things that resonate with me? I started to explore more of the show and realized that he was talking about your physical vehicle, your mindset and positive living, plus the food you put into your body. On his TV show, he engaged with his audience and made them feel like there was a personal connection. I also found out he had studied anatomy and became a chiropractor. When I met him face to face, his spirit really came out. He's a coach, a teacher, trainer, a **scientist**, a business person, author, motivating speaker, but it was his ability to inspire others that impacted me greatly.

He exuded more of a celebration of what the body can do and a celebration for life. I saw the celebration for exercise, nutrition and the brain. You still see that within Elaine today. She carries the spirit of Jack and what he stood for.

He was on a **mission** to change how people think, how they live, how they eat, how they exercise. In some ways, he was a **contrarian** which can be lonely as a leader. Imagine if your ideas and information that you're going to proliferate are quite different, are very different from what most of society and businesses are doing and so on. He never deviated from his mission.

Peter Twist
NHL consultant, author, speaker, trainer and cancer survivor

Cathe Friedrich In life there are those that find their passion and follow the path that it leads them on and then there are those that lay the path for others to follow. This is true of Jack LaLanne. Jack didn't fall into a life of fitness, he created a life of fitness. The steps he took are what helped to form the foundation for all fitness professionals that followed. I, like Jack, followed my passion even though the naysayers were against it. Without his contributions to the industry, I don't believe that my life and career would have been the same. I know that I owe a lot to him every time I do a jumping "jack," everytime I walk into my own health club, every time I teach a group of people what the face of fitness and wellness looks like.

Cathe Friedrich
Fitness entrepreneur and innovator

Todd Durkin My path into the fitness industry was inspired from working out at Jack LaLanne's gym during high school and college.

When I had the chance to meet Jack at one of the IDEA World shows, I thought I wanted to be like him. This is the guy you emulated. His mindset and physicality was awe-inspiring. We in the fitness industry should put a pioneer like Jack LaLanne on our shoulders. We need to make sure the younger generation of trainers, fit pros, fitness enthusiasts, weekend warriors, and many others know who Jack LaLanne was and how his legacy will live forever. Jack was a chiropractor. He didn't practice formally because of the stigma of the medical community. He also became a pioneer through his time studying nutrition. He really looked at sugar and what it does to the brain 50+ years before this research was accepted by many doctors, and other men and women who are leading the way today.

You talk about mindset. The dozens of different physical feats that Jack did are impossible if you don't get your mind right. Jack epitomized the idea of a mind-right maniac. He was a stud. He's the kind of guy that I still want to be. To the day he died, Jack was swimming, he was lifting, he was working out. He maximized life.

Todd Durkin
Internationally recognized strength, speed and conditioning coach, personal trainer, motivational speaker, author

Allen Joe (left) and Bruce Lee

Allen Joe (as told by Lana Kim) Jack's influence crosses many boundaries. In 1936, Allen Joe was 13 years old. He was a very skinny kid and wanted to learn how to lift weights. His mentor, Ed Yarick, whom he met through his childhood friend, James Lee, knew Jack LaLanne. Allen learned from Jack LaLanne and Jack eventually became a major influence in Allen's life. When you see the sculptured body of Bruce Lee in the movies, it was Allen Joe who trained Bruce in bodybuilding techniques and it was Jack LaLanne who trained Allen Joe. Bruce was not dedicating much of his fitness routine to weight training, so Allen Joe introduced Bruce to using weights along with nutrition, protein shakes, and juices.

Jack would never say, "Allen, you have to exercise every day, you have to do the weights, what is your diet?" Jack simply led by example and his legacy lived in Allen Joe for 95 years.

Allen Joe
Trainer

Harry & Sarah Sneider My husband Harry and I brought Olympic medalist Dwight Stones to Jack and Elaine's home in 1980. We shared a system Harry and I developed using a mini-trampoline and soft hand-held weights. Jack endorsed our new system and gave us photos to use in our book, "Harry and Sarah Sneiders' Olympic Trainer." Jack enjoyed competing with Dwight doing chin-ups, leg extensions and more, and Jack always won those friendly competitions.

In 1992, he also enjoyed demonstrating weight training to an audience at the Great American Workout on The White House lawn presented by President George H.W. Bush and Arnold Schwarzenegger. Also in attendance were Muhammad Ali, Denise Austin and other fitness industry leaders.

Jack told us we could do some great things as trainers and to strive for bigger and better things. He was a wonderful motivator and encourager and told us, "Anything is possible, you can make it happen."

Dr. Harry & Sarah Sneider
Creator Resistive Rebounding, Olympic Trainer

Guy Steele Jack and Elaine walked into my office and Jack plunked down $10,000.00 to invest. He said, "I've never been an investor. What can you do with this?" Jack knew what he wanted and had the confidence to attain it. I never considered the importance of exercise. I never thought I could ever run a marathon, thinking it was beyond my ability. But because of Jack's motivation, and inspiration, instilling confidence in those he met, I started running. I ran two marathons in one year, completed a hundred mile bike ride with my wife, Lily, and at 65 and, as I write this, I'm going to ride a bike 350 miles in 10 days.

Jack inspired me when he said, "I believe in vigorous, daily, systematic exercise. I'm usually up each day at 3:30 a.m. I hit the gym at 4 a.m. I'm out at 6:30 a.m. I do it seven days a week and have ever since I can remember. It's very easy to rationalize and say, I didn't get enough sleep or I'm too busy or I've got this little ache or pain. It's tough. It's hard. The good thing is when I'm finished, I look at myself in the mirror and say, Jack, you've done it again!" WOW! Those words were inspiring enough to change my life.

Guy Steele
Investment Broker

Anibal Lopez I wanted to be like Jack. He was a positive role model, and his longevity is something I strive for.

Anibal Lopez
Mr. America 1978 (WBBG)

Judi Sheppard Missett I remember seeing Jack first on TV with his dog when I was a little girl. I always thought he was kind of cool to be doing exercise on TV. I didn't see anyone else doing that. I was a dancer so I was used to doing movement, but I thought it was great that grown-ups had something so fun and dynamic to do for exercise.

Years later when I met him, I felt like I was meeting an icon. He always had such energy and enthusiasm. No matter where we were, whether it was at a governor's or president's council meetings or, really, *any* kind of function, you could always depend on Jack to get the room and crowd filled with energy. He was never embarrassed to just jump up and start moving.

Judi Sheppard Missett
Founder of Jazzercise

Tony Horton The short three and half minute conversation I had with Jack at the airport had a huge impact on me. It sparked a shift in the direction my life would go. In those days fitness training wasn't my main focus. I wanted to be an actor. Driving all over town training people back then was just a way to survive and pay my bills. The limelight, red carpets, and sound stages were to be my future. Everything changed after I had trained Tom Petty for four months prior to one of his tours. He was transformed. He had tons of energy on stage, his voice sounded better than ever, and the cool thing was, I helped make that happen.

It was decision time for me. Did I want to continue to pursue this acting career or help more people get strong, be healthy and improve their lives. It turns out that my days on a stage, in acting classes, and performing were all components to my success as a fitness trainer.

I was able to help millions of people around the world improve the quality of their lives.

My airport conversation was the one and only meeting that I ever had with Jack. I've met with Elaine a few times, and really enjoyed listening to her talk about Jack and their history together. Elaine and I were both blown away that there are so many young people who've never heard of Jack. I say his name and they have no idea who he was. And when you explain to people who he was and what his accomplishments were, they don't believe you.

I have this amazing newspaper article from the early days at Muscle Beach in Santa Monica that shows one of Jack's buddies in a back bend in the sand, with Jack and three other guys standing stacked on top of each other. You look at that photo and ask, "Is that photoshopped?" Nope, this was Cirque du Soleil decades before there was a Cirque du Soleil. Without Jack and without all his accomplishments and charisma, a lot of people world wide wouldn't be in shape today. Jack's inventions alone changed the gym industry. He's the John Glenn, the George Washington of health, wellness and fitness. That's the impact that he's had on me and other people like me, and the impact that we've all had on tens of millions of people around the world.

To this day I remind folks that these things actually happened. He was actually a real life Superman. What we have in common is the ability to transcend the importance of health and fitness in a fun and authentic way.

Tony Horton
2016 winner of the Jack LaLanne Award
through Idea World, Creator of P90X program

Ricky Suzuki Jack is without a doubt The Founder, The Pioneer, The Godfather and The Single Most Influential Person of the fitness industry. He had such a major impact on so many lives. Not only on fitness and nutrition, but also with his kind words of wisdom and his philosophies on life to just be a better person. I can still remember watching Jack and Happy on our black and white TV in the early 60s when I was still a little turd. Jack always liked my arms. He said, "I can tell by your body structure and muscle definition that you don't take steroids. You did it the right way, Ricky." He told me I grew up in the wrong era. Jack said, "In the 50s and 60s, if you had 16 inch arms you were somebody, and your arms are much bigger than that." When I have a good day at the gym, I always say to myself, Jack would be proud. Jack had a way of making every person he met feel special. And his zest and enthusiasm for life was very contagious. I would like to thank Jack, Elaine and Danny for a friendship that I will always cherish. Jack's legacy will live on forever and I will dedicate the rest of my life to make sure that continues. But I must say, Jack could have never gotten as far as he did without the guidance of his beautiful wife Elaine. Like they say, behind every great man, there's a greater woman.

Ricky Suzuki
Promoter of Hawaiian Islands BodyBuilding Championships

Clark Bartram I remember the day Jack walked onto the set of my television show, American Health & Fitness. I was introducing him, and the guest had no clue that I was bringing out the pioneer of the health and fitness movement. When Jack walked out, both she and I were nearly speechless and honored to be talking to the man who brought fitness to the world through television. Now he was on my show! How did this happen? How was I so lucky for this to be happening?

The impact he had on me, that day, and for many more to come, has led me to the place I'm at today.

Jack's words ruminate in my mind as I speak to men on my podcast, and encourage them to live healthy lives. He would tell me, "Clark, just keep your message simple and lead by example. Fitness isn't that complicated."

I am so grateful and honored to have worked with Jack on many occasions and each time was more special than the last.

Clark Bartram
Master Trainer for International Sports Science Association,
Marine, Fitness Trainer, Author

Legacy

Clint Eastwood *The following is Clint Eastwood's interview from Tri Star's "Anything is Possible" tribute to Jack LaLanne commemorating his 100ᵗʰ Birthday.*

When I was in junior high, Jack LaLanne came to our school and did a demonstration of hand balancing and performing a handstand with blocks. He built them all the way up behind the curtains, up into the ceiling, then back down again. He did all these crazy things.

In those days I didn't work out a lot and to see this guy who was very athletic and strong do all these things; it was amazing. In fact, a lot of kids started going to his gym in downtown Oakland and I did occasionally. He was a terrific guy. We were inspired but It was kind of foreign to us. This was in the 1940s. Strongmen were thought of as circus performers and people who lifted weights would get muscle bound and couldn't do anything else. People didn't watch what they ate--mostly white bread sandwiches, pot roasts, lots of grease and overcooked vegetables. Jack was the pioneer to change all of that.

I got to know him years later, too when I got into the movie business. He came down to LA and started doing his television show wearing a jumpsuit. He

Jack's student, Jim Drinkward, champion bodybuilder and gymnast, spotting. Jim was 6 ft 4. Jack often said that Jim was unusual because there were very few champion gymnasts that tall.

was often called Jumping Jack. I remember, it was great. He was an evangelist as far as lifestyle and exercise were concerned. At that time he was the leading guy and became the guru of it. He advocated moderation and taking care of yourself to have a good quality of life. He could sell whatever he believed in and if someone said they could do 1000 pushups he would do 1500. He was also a great swimmer, towed boats, hands, and feet cuffed, from Alcatraz to San Francisco.

He lived his lifestyle way up into his nineties. He was a guru!

Clint Eastwood
American film actor, film director, producer, composer

Keith Morrison Jack's legacy is the recognition that anybody, a 95-year old, a 75 pound overweight middle-aged woman or man, anyone, can be healthy and happier and more engaged with life, by following some of the precepts (exercise, proper nutrition and positive thinking) that he cared about so much.

Keith Morrison
Dateline NBC Correspondent

Tosca Reno When I think about legacy work, I think about the value and the enduring quality. When we are a 'way show-er' or a disrupter we break systems. Jack had a mainstream way of making fitness acceptable. Bodybuilding is still very niche, not everybody is doing it, although fitness people are kind of bodybuilders. Jack kept it to a place where the masses could dine at the table and learn and partake. He did it not just through exercise, but through talking about the principles of wellness that still stand the test of time today, so that's also part of legacy work. Legacy work changes the world, and he did that.

Tosca Reno
Author, Creator and founder of Eat Clean books, published by Robert Kennedy

Ed Labowitz Dan Doyle, Elaine's son and Jack's step son, and I first met as 11 year-olds in Boy Scout Troop 111, Hollywood, California in 1959. Being a friend of Dan meant being a friend of Elaine and Jack. Of course, all of the scouts knew who Jack was and, in my case, Jack meant even more; my mother watched Jack's show whenever she could, so she could exercise when she was not working with my father in their grocery store on Hollywood Boulevard. Dan and I remained friends through high school, after which we went our separate ways.

When we met again in 2003, for the 100th anniversary celebration of the founding of Hollywood High School, I had been an entertainment lawyer in Los Angeles for 30 years and Dan a producer and director and, along with Elaine, had been handling the digitization of Jack's original television shows. Dan and I renewed our friendship. Shortly after, Jack and Elaine engaged me as their lawyer for their company.

It was an honor, privilege, and inspiration to work with Jack, Elaine, and Dan from that moment until Jack's passing, and continuing to this day with Elaine, Dan, and Jon LaLanne. I remain in awe of Jack's vision and steadfastness to the principle that everyone can help themselves to be and remain fit -- and to his and Elaine's great sense of humor and positive attitudes.

Ed Labowicz
Family Attorney

Peter Twist Jack's legacy in the fitness industry is about being an effective communicator, inspiring people, teaching them how to simplify complex ideas. Outside of the fitness industry, he leaves a legacy of raising the expectations of what is possible. Jack encouraged people to "own the process" and have positive self-talk. He empowered people and that's an important legacy.

Peter Twist
NHL consultant, author, speaker, trainer and cancer survivor

Tamilee Webb Jack was a pioneer. He's the godfather of fitness. He broke down the walls for all of us in the fitness industry. His inspiration, his strength, both physical and mental was second to none. He had such a good balance of the mental and physical. Everything was balanced, and his persistence was amazing too. When he says, "I'm going to do this," he's going to do it. His legacy will live on forever.

Tamilee Webb
Hall of Fame Fitness Instructor and creator of "Buns of Steel" fitness program series

Mark Rothstein His legacy is that we try to attain and think about each and every day we wake up and go to work and have a positive impact on people. He was a humble man and always had time to converse with people. I remember my first conversation with him, when he said, Mark, you have to work to live. He always had a way of saying things so profoundly but yet so important and vital to a good quality of life.

Jack's integrity was impeccable and his passion for fitness and encouraging everyone to spread the word was consistent. We call him "The Godfather of Fitness," and that's an apropos statement. He was easily 50 years ahead of his time. He was a trendsetter. He was a role model. He was an inspirer. He was my all-time mentor.

Mark Rothstein
Two Guinness World Records for endurance rope jumping,
National Fitness Hall of Fame, presenter, and speaker

Kathy Smith His legacy is that he stood for empowering people to be the best they could be. And that empowerment process kept him and his vision very directed. He was value-based. He believed in the goodness of people, he believed in the potential of everyone. And he really developed a company that never swayed or swerved away from what his values were.

Kathy Smith
Fitness Entrepeneur, podcaster, host of Alive and Well TV show

Gilad Janklowic Besides the legacy that he left in the fitness industry, to me, as a fitness person who's involved with the public, is the encouragement that he gave to the average viewer at home through his TV show, and further through his personality. He was highly approachable. Jack had a special way of connecting with people. He just talked to them face to face, eye to eye, and that's what people remember.

Gilad Janklowic
Creator of ESPN TV fitness show 'Bodies in Motion',
'Basic Training the Workout' and 'Total Body Sculpt with Gilad'

Jaime Brenkus I talk about the 3D system: discipline, dedication and determination in one of my books. Jack lived those principles and was my inspiration. He was the voice of reason when it came to fitness, health and lifestyle. Jack's legacy is also about making people aware of their responsibility to their body. He would say, "You have to train your body. That's your responsibility. It's incumbent upon you to take care of your own machine." He would remind people that they're never out of the race. Your age doesn't matter, you can start today and do *something*. His approach was that you have to, and here's how you CAN. To me, that approach is just beautiful, and what legacy is all about. Jack's legacy will live on forever, through his **work ethic, positivity** and **inclusivity.** His dedication to his craft was unmatched. There will never be another one like him.

Jaime Brenkus
Co-Author with Elaine LaLanne, "If You Want to Live, MOVE.
Putting the Boom back in Bommers" Creator of "8-Minute Abs" video series

Dr. Fabrizio Mancini Jack's legacy as fitness expert came at a time when health and wellness were not popular. He was creative in the way he messaged us-- it was practical, simple to implement, not complicated. I truly feel that in the early days when Jack began to promote the lifestyle of health and wellness, it was more than just fitness. He saw in us our potential. As a **loving** person he captured unconditional love, and he kept wanting to remind us of that throughout his life, no matter what limitations others put on him. He was trying to educate people into lifestyle choices, not only nutrition, but also not smoking. In those days, it was very prevalent that most people, especially celebrities and influencers, were big smokers. Jack really took a position that was non-conventional. He pushed boundaries and achieved things that most people have never done. He was **persistent** because he never gave up on his mission and impacted millions of people around the world. He will be remembered as the Father of Wellness.

Dr. Fabrizio Mancini
Internationally acclaimed chiropractor, bilingual speaker, author,
educator, philanthropist; and former president of Parker University

Tony Little His legacy to the world was he cared about people. He cared about their fitness. He cared about their energy. He cared about their lives. His legacy was that he touched millions and millions of people, and he cared about every one of them.

Tony Little
Certified Personal Trainer, Physical Fitness Specialist and
former National Bodybuilding Champion, HSN spokesperson

Dion Jackson "Be an example." That was Jack's answer when I first met him at the opening of his gym in Inglewood, CA in the 1970s and asked for his advice. I knew then that I wanted to be just like him. He gave me something I knew I could do. In the long run, as people are starting to synthesize and sift through those who are {working in the fitness industry} only to make money, they'll look back and admire

{Jack}, because he was a real person. He could have easily laid back, relaxed and kicked it in, but he was current. Jack taught me to change the workout every 30 days. You have to be versatile. If I could say three words back to him, I would tell him he's an **Extreme Fitness Entertainer.** He didn't accept the normal. He pushed himself, challenged himself, documented himself, videotaped himself, had his own show. He sang, he had the dog, he had the stick, the chair, he danced. He always ended his whole show with a song. He made fitness entertaining. The best way to honor a man is to do his work when he's not around. He was my real life hero.

Dion Jackson
Mega-Celebrity
Certified Personal Fitness Trainer, Fitness Philanthropist, and Group Instructor

Forbes Riley I've been around since the dawn of infomercials and when I got a call to do a juicer infomercial with Jack LaLanne, I made sure I was in shape after just having twins. This developed into not only making infomercials for the Jack LaLanne Power Juicer (and we sold tons during an 8-year period) but a friendship that has lasted to this day.

It began in a dressing room in Toronto in 2002 when we first met. Jack and "Lala" as he called her, were electrifying. It was love at first sight. The magnetism and energy was dynamic. I could tell this man loved people. Over the years I got to know them intimately, how they lived and how they loved people. We spent many hours on set, many dinners, many parties, and I have made numerous visits to their home. Jack had a light, a glow about him. His energy affected everyone. He never put anybody down, practiced what he preached and never, ever, deviated from his eating habits or exercise.

His legacy is represented in everyone that is running around in a fitness outfit or on social media representing fitness. He laid the path. His message was pure and simple--"fitness is your birthright." He changed my entire life!

I will also give a love shout out to my mother from another mother. Elaine has become one of my greatest all time friends and one of my role models. She stood next to, behind and around her man. I watched for years how Lala was a little bit in the shadow, but she had her own sense. And she was 100% committed to Jack and their mission: health is available for everyone. They were always together. It was the most beautiful testament to love. This spunky, amazing, committed woman who can still feel her husband, is her own entity. She, at 95, is still zipping around and entertaining guests in her home. My family and I have spent many happy hours there. Elaine is never going to get old. Her training, her love for him, his love from her will never let her get old. Because of the passion, love and commitment for their mission, the idea of health, vibrancy, and vitality can live forever.

Forbes Riley
Author, lifestyle expert, creator of the Spin Gym, award winning TV host, over 15 years with Jack LaLanne Power Juicer Infomercials.

Eric the Trainer (Eric Fleishman) I've tried to emulate Jack to the best of my ability. My goal was to be a modern day version of Jack LaLanne. When I think about Jack, I think about his excellence and his drive and his charisma, but I also think about the fact that he is essentially an ambassador of health and fitness to the common man. He is not some unattainable bodybuilder on the top of a mountain looking like Hercules. He's the guy who, with a big smile on his face and enthusiasm, reached his hand out to the average American and said, "Come with me on this journey. I'll show you how to go, and we'll have a great time." When I think about Jack LaLanne, I think about seven words: **What Can I Do For You Today**? He lived a service-based life, as opposed to a self-serving life. There's a big difference. When I wake up every day, I leap out of bed excited to help people that day. I think to myself, what can I do today to help people look better, feel better, live a better life as a service-based individual? I learned that from the great Jack LaLanne.

Eric the Trainer Fleishman
Hollywood Physique Expert, contributor to *Fitness and Muscle* magazine

Todd Durkin Jack's legacy is all about your health and fitness which will always need to be paramount to a great life. Jack lived and breathed fitness. His legacy is the commitment, the perseverance, the discipline to always put your health and fitness first. Jack LaLanne lived his life that way. He said, 'If man makes it, don't eat it. 'If it tastes good, spit it out.' These are the things, when you look back, went way beyond his years, before health and fitness was even in vogue. He made it vogue.

Todd Durkin
Internationally recognized strength, speed and conditioning coach,
personal trainer, motivational speaker, author

Robert A. Finkelstein I couldn't believe how disciplined Jack was, what incredible shape he was in, and what energy he had. I grew up watching him and so it was such a treat to finally meet Jack and Elaine. He brought so much inspiration to so many lives and now Elaine continues to keep his legacy alive. Bravo, bravo, bravo!

If you grew up in Southern California as a child there were a few ubiquitous television programs such as Howdy Doody, Beanie and Cecil, the Mouseketeers, and Jack LaLanne. Sixty years later (I am 73), this older guy doing push-ups and advocating a healthy lifestyle remains a beacon of inspiration for pursuing a life balance of exercise and healthy eating. Jack and Elaine LaLanne's contribution to the health of an aging generation is a hidden phenomenon. It is an honor to contribute to the celebration and continuing recognition of Jack and Elaine LaLanne.

Robert Finkelstein
Attorney, Co-Chairman of Frank Sinatra Enterprises

Jay Blahnik One of my first IDEA conventions was in 1982 and Jack was speaking. After hearing Jack speak, I realized he was a man, in the later part of his career, who still had a lot of passion about health, fitness, and nutrition. He was a motivator and an educator. He made these things his career and influenced so many people. I took the very first personal trainer certification exam a few years later.

Meeting Jack at the tail-end of the convention helped change the trajectory of my life. I thought Jack had superpowers. He taught me the power of storytelling, marketing and showcasing what you are passionate about to inspire others. He understood the impact and influence of social media before it even existed.

Jack's legacy could be that he was the one individual who communicated fitness, nutrition, wellbeing and mindset. He wanted everyone to extend their years, have independence in their life, a better state of mind, and a positive attitude. The by-product was that you might like your body, and it might look better. He made *health* the guiding principle.

In an industry that can often distort fact from fiction, Jack was honest from the beginning right to the end, sometimes even bluntly and brutally honest. He didn't want to sugar coat it. When he shared his pearls of wisdom about what health and fitness meant, he was honest in a way that helped people understand that it wasn't complicated, and even though he understood the science behind it, there were simple, evergreen principles, and he brought them to the forefront.

He understood that to motivate and educate, you have to be entertaining. Truth is we have humor and we have feelings and emotions for a reason as a species. He understood how to pique their interests, grab their attention, tell them the right story, and make them laugh. He took a very serious subject and knew how to make it not medical, not intimidating, but entertaining. The industry has been trying to keep up with that legacy ever since.

Jay Blahnik
Fitness instructor, trainer, consultant, author, program developer,
and the Senior Director of Fitness for Health technologies for Apple Inc.
Recipient of 2018 IDEA Jack LaLanne Award

CONCLUSION

Life is great when you're in shape. - LaLanne-ism

One of Jack's quips was, "I can't die. It would wreck my image." We're sure of one thing in life - death is certain. And while that thought is undoubtedly ominous for some, Jack didn't approach life "waiting to die." He challenged himself, his family, and millions worldwide to embrace today with an unwavering credence rooted in pride and discipline.

To anyone that knew Jack, his belief in pride and discipline was far from some stereotypical drill sergeant or an overbearing 4 AM exercise regime. Of his most enduring legacies were his sense of humor, a holistic take on life, and how visualization can help you achieve whatever it is you set out to do. Elaine, Jack's loving wife, observed this last point early on in their relationship, remarking on his innate inclination for visualization as something unique and special. Regardless of whether it was redecorating the living room or performing one of his numerous feats, Jack visualized a transformed living room in just the same way he visualized himself in sub-optimal temperatures, battling the Pacific's currents and reaching shore in one piece. He argued (quite convincingly) that if you can't visualize yourself fulfilling whatever it is you set out to do, why in the heck even attempt it?

Many influential people who contributed to this book championed his message. Some suggest Jack's upbringing played a significant role in his ultimate success. As a weak kid who subsisted on sugar and junk food, had it not been for this inauspicious beginning, he would not have needed to turn things around and forge a new path. Who knows, but one thing's for certain - Jack understood the power of self-determination and corrective action. He was moved by five words as a young boy, *"You can be born again."* In many respects, Jack was born again and went on to play a pioneering role in promoting exercise and healthy living to his loyal followers.

Jack opened the first modern health spa and was also the first to have a weight loss instant breakfast meal replacement drink, way back in 1956! Jack used chairs, books, doorknobs, door jams, walls, and water bottles to break a sweat. Excuses bounced off Jack like flies on a windshield. The notion that someone couldn't work-out for lack of weights, a gym membership, etc., was nonsensical. But more than simply convincing people about the benefits of exercise, Jack believed that exercise, remaining fit and healthy, was the key to success in anything.

A poorly tuned body could never attempt to succeed in anything physically or academically oriented because the mind is part of the body. If the body is sluggish and overweight, the mind naturally follows. It is no coincidence that the great athletes were also great scholars in ancient Greek and Roman times. Jack reminded the naysayers of this every chance he got.

Jack was a man who conquered the force within, found his calling in life, and pursued it with a passion. He was proud of who he was, what he stood for, and employed the discipline necessary to carry out his actions. With an eternal smile, a wry wit, and a zest for enjoying every breathing minute on God's green Earth, Jack is off to rest, but even that sounds crazy to those who knew him.

Greg Justice

I pretty much summed up Jack in my forward, however, I would like to conclude with a few anecdotes.

Although he called his viewers students, he was a student, always learning something new, looking at life objectively and loved to hear other people's stories. During our personal appearances, when signing autographs, he would love to ask each person, in line, about their life and was totally interested in each one. If our schedule permitted, he would spend hours until the last one left. However, if we had to catch a plane, I would have to inform him, "Jack! The plane isn't going to wait for us!" Consequently, I would go down the line of those who were still waiting and get their names and addresses to send them a picture. On the way out he would say hello and shake their hands. He always took time for everyone whether it be on the street or in a restaurant. He was not a complainer, anything went wrong, he blamed himself.

Jack was basically shy and had to conquer that notion throughout his life. I believe the fervor he had for his life changing experience as a teenager, his belief in his profession, and his connection with the public, helped conquer that shyness, subsequently, helping others to conquer their afflictions.

There are so many facets to Jack. He was funny, dedicated, disciplined, steadfast and stellar. This book gives you an insight, but here is how Jack summed up himself, "When I play, I play for keeps and tear the grass in great big heaps!"

Elaine "LaLa" LaLanne

Conquering the Force Within

Therefore, I would say that this is of prime importance. In my case, I had to make a profession out of what I believed in because there were no **modern** health spas when I started business in 1936.

Conquering the force within me began at age 15 when I was a junk food junkie, a sugarholic. I had boils, pimples, arch supports, and glasses. I was weak, sick, and had to drop out of school for six months. That's when I met Paul Bragg, at his lecture. I was inspired when he said, "I don't care what your age is, I don't care what your physical condition is, you can be reborn again." I've told this story many times but those words were, and are, still embedded in my brain! I believed I could reach my goals; to have a healthy body and play sports. Back in school, I became captain of the football team, played baseball, and in my weight class, became an AAU Wrestling champion. My enthusiasm propelled me to set up a gym in my backyard and to invent equipment of my own design. While still in high school, I had firemen and policemen working out in my backyard. I would put them on a specific, individual program of exercise and keep check on their progress. Believing in myself was my force within, and the force that drove me to attend college and go into medicine. However, I decided I needed to help people before they got sick.

In 1936 there were gyms for bodybuilders that were often called "sweat boxes" where the bodybuilders worked out with mostly barbells and dumbbells. Also there were boxing and wrestling gyms. I wanted people to work out in a nice atmosphere; rugs on the floor, plants all around, clean block glass showers, steam baths, and healthy food. So I opened just such a place with the health food store on the first floor and the gym on the second. It was located on 14th street in Oakland. I paid $45 a month rent.

People made fun of me saying that there was some crackpot muscleman who was charging people to exercise; doctors were saying don't go to Jack LaLanne's because you would be muscle-bound. I was called a nut and a charlatan so I went to the local high schools in tight T-shirts and talked to the skinny kids and the fat kids about working out and eating right. I had to sell their parents on the idea. The kids got such great results that the parents started coming, too.

To keep my clients interested from time to time I would invent a new piece of equipment; that's how the first pulley machine, using cables, came into being. I also invented the first weight selector, leg extension and squat machine. In the late 1930's and early 40's, I never thought to patent anything, and now those same concepts are used all over the world.

I continued to study and graduated from Chiropractic college. However, by that time I was working with the MD's and because of the conflicts between Chiropractors and the MD's at the time, I kept my degree to myself.

By the time 1951 rolled around television was in its infancy. I was asked to do a television show on exercise and nutrition. To help pay for the TV time I developed the first powdered energy drink, called Instant Breakfast and the first rubber stretcher, the Glamour Stretcher. The show was syndicated, went nationwide, and ran for over 34 years.

Today my force within drives me to continue to read, study, and learn. It is important you don't go through life with your blinders on. Be multi-faceted, learn about a variety of things; geography, math, social graces, languages and anything and everything that interests you. The more you expand your mind and your body, the longer you're going to live, the happier and more successful you are going to be.

It is most gratifying to me to see that everything I was preaching and advocating over 60 years ago; not only in exercise but nutrition, is coming into fruition. Back then I was called a crackpot, a nut and a charlatan. Today I am an authority.

Remember, be curious, keep learning, keep stretching, keep striving. The stars are your limit! Anything in life is possible. Practice **Pride and Discipline**. Practice what you preach. Believe in what you're doing. Make it happen!

Yours in Good Health,

Jack LaLanne

SECTION EIGHT

Timeline

"Work at living and you don't have to die tomorrow." - LaLanne-ism

1914: Born in San Francisco, September 16. Jack's journey begins.

Left: All dressed up. *Right:* Precocious Jack trying to climb in horse trough at Grandpa's Sheep Ranch, Bakersfield, CA.

1930: Age 16. One year after learning about the benefits of weights.

1932: Age 18. Making progress with his physique and with the girls.

1935: Age 21. The picture above was used in the June 1936 Strength & Health magazine with the caption, "Here is a man who would upset a competitor in any contest for the World's Best Built Man."

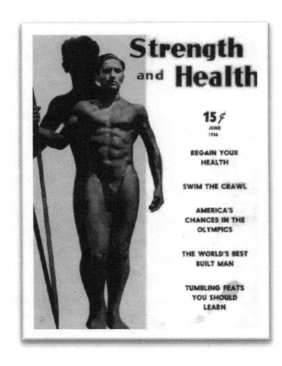

JACK LALANNE

1936: Just before his 22nd birthday. Opened the first modern fitness club called *Jack LaLanne's Physical Culture Studio*. He pioneered the first selectorcize weight apparatus and pulley exercise machines, many of which are used in gyms today. *Left:* Weight room in Jack's gym. *Right:* Jack's office at his physical culture studio.

2-1-2000

Dear Jack,

Would you kindly authenticate the following facts of History of this enclosed pictured 12 foot paddleboard as it was relayed to me in 1970 by the former 1939 Mr. California, and highly respected physical culturist Mr. Carl Cathy of Oakland Calif.

Carl informed me that this paddleboard was one (1) of a pair that you, and he used for transportation, and physical recreation on the San Francisco Bay during the 1930's And 1940's while living on a houseboat docked in Alameda Calif.

In addition to the above history Carl indicated that this paddleboard was used by yourself, he, And Ed Yarik in an exhibition canoe, and paddleboard race against the Hawaiin canoe racing team lead

- 2 -

by the great swimming and surfing legend Duke Kahanamoku during the 1939 Worlds Fair held at Treasure Island in the San Francisco Bay. Your verification of these facts will be greatly appreciated.

Yours in Health,
Your friend,
Kevin J. O'Connell
Duncans Mills, Calif.

Authenticated by: Jack LaLanne Feb 5 2000

1938-1939: Age 24-25. This paddleboard was used during the 1939 World's Fair as well as for recreation by Jack LaLanne. Kevin O'Connell (pictured) heard stories about Jack, Carl Cathy and Ed Yarik using the paddleboard in exhibition races against world reknowned surfer, Duke Kahanamoku. Kevin asked Jack to authenticate the stories he had heard. Letter and photos provided by Margaret O'Connell.

1944: Age 30. World War II. Jack returned from Guadal Canal and Suva to US Naval Hospital in Sun Valley Idaho where he set up a fitness program to rehabilitate the wounded. During his tenure he performed 100 unsupported full handstand press-ups in five minutes and fifty-seven seconds.

Left: 100 handstand press-ups. *Right:* US Navy Certification.

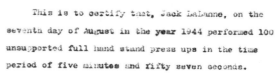

NNRSH—FORM 22
(1935)

U. S. NAVAL HOSPITAL

Sun Valley, Idaho

This is to certify that, Jack LaLanne, on the seventh day of August in the year 1944 performed 100 unsupported full hand stand press ups in the time period of five minutes and fifty seven seconds.

First witness and timekeeper for the event being Lt.(jg) Ralph A. Mazzei USNR.

Second witness and scorekeeper for the event being Joseph P. Stalego Phm.2/c USNR.

1st witness: *Ralph A. Mazzei*
Ralph A. Mazzei
Lt.(jg) USNR
Physical Training Officer
U.S. Naval Convalescent Hospital
Sun Valley, Idaho

2nd witness: *Joseph P. Stalego PHM 2/c*
Joseph P. Stalego Phm.2/c USNR
Physical Instructor

1947-1949: Age 33-35. Jack never gave up on his training. During his life he embraced innumerable articles and covers of magazines. At age 33 his waist was 27 inches. Chest 48 inches. The July 1949 issue of Muscle Power Magazine (pictured right), featured one of Jack's students, Norman Marks—Mr. California, gym owner, chiropractor and one of Jack's first students. The issue also included a two page article by Joe Weider, and pictorial review of the Most Elaborate Gym in the U.S.A. The photos were shot by noted physique photographer, Russ Warner, also a student of Jack and announcer for The Jack LaLanne TV shows.

1949: Age 35. Jack being pulled out of the water by one of his students after swimming across San Francisco Bay from Oakland to San Francisco, California. Jack's brother, Norman looks on.

1951: Age 37. Jack began the 34-year run of his TV program at KGO-TV San Francisco. Jack would often hold fitness classes during lunchtime. Elaine, (center), participated, and was hooked on fitness, then two year later, hooked on Jack.

1954: Age 40. Jack explaining to his students on TV his plans to swim the length of the San Francisco Golden Gate Bridge *underwater* with 140 pounds of equipment, including two air tanks. He barely made it before the air ran out.

1955: Age 41. Jack swam handcuffed in shark infested waters, from Alcatraz Island to Fisherman's Wharf in San Francisco.

"News columnist take on it."

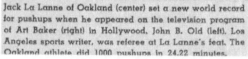

Jack La Lanne of Oakland (center) set a new world record for pushups when he appeared on the television program of Art Baker (right) in Hollywood. John B. Old (left), Los Angeles sports writer, was referee at La Lanne's feat. The Oakland athlete did 1000 pushups in 24.22 minutes.

1956: Age 42. Breaking the current record on live television, Jack performed 1033 pushups in 23 minutes on ABC TV's national Art Baker "You Asked for It" program. Left: Art Baker congratulating Jack. Below: Pushups during the show.

1957: Age 43. Against strong winds, Jack attempted to ski on one ski behind a helicopter to the Farallon Islands and back. 15 miles en route, Rick, of Rick Helicopters, told co-pilot for the day, Elaine, that due to strong winds, it would be impossible to return from the desolate islands because they were using too much fuel fighting the strong winds. She immediately made the decision to turn around. The feat ended up being 32 miles instead of 64 miles. Jack called it his "half a feat." Elaine's note: "As on every feat, I was there and IT WASN'T EASY!"

Jack, ready to go.

Happy crew to be back safe.

1958: Age 44. In 9 and half hours, Jack paddled all night on this 10-foot Longboard designed by legendary surf industry pioneer, Jack O'Neill, from the Farallon Islands into San Francisco Bay. A distance of 32 miles.

1959: Age 45. Relocated to Los Angeles and syndicated his popular Jack LaLanne Show nationwide. Not known in Hollywood as he was in San Francisco, note the misspelling of his last name. That was soon to change.

Jack with his two favorite TV stars, Happy (on the right) and Smiley (left). As the years rolled by Chuckles and WALTER (We All Love To Exercise Regularly) were added to the program.

Jack utilizing his favorite prop, the chair!

1959: Age 45. Breaking another World Record, Jack completed 1,000 push-ups and 1,000 chin-ups in an hour and 22 minutes.

1961-1969: Age 47-55. Jack continued to film new episodes of his exercise shows, tour the country lecturing, and make guest appearances on major TV shows.

Jack doing a live show in New York.

To accommodate the large crowd, Jack lectured in a movie theatre in the Midwest.

Jack on "The Lucy Show" with his dog, Happy.

Jack on "The Steve Allen Show" with Bob Newhart and Tim Conway demonstrating Face-A-Tonics.

1969: Age 55. While still doing his TV shows, Jack had the opportunity to open a national chain of Jack LaLanne spas. He traveled extensively to help kick it off. The chain grew to be the largest of its kind during that period.

1974: Age 60. Jack again swam from Alcatraz to Fisherman's Wharf in San Francisco. This time his hands and feet were shacked as he pulled a 1,000-pound boat.

Jack (white swim cap) on press boat.

En route from Alcatraz

Got caught in the dock pilings and released himself without help.

Whew! Coming out of the water.

1975: Age 61. Jack swam the length of the Golden Gate Bridge underwater for a second time. This time not only was he was handcuffed, his feet were shackled. Instead of air tanks strapped to his back, air was fed through a tube from a boat above water. His son, Jon Allen, 14 years old at the time, went down periodically to check on him. *Left:* Handcuffed and feet shackled. *Right:* Elaine greeting Jack, and Jon Allen as they emerged from the water.

1976: Age 62. In Long Beach, California Jack pulled 76 people in 13 boats, the Queen Mary Mile while hand-cuffed and feet shackled to celebrate the "Spirit of 76", 200 year bicentennial.

1979: Age 65. Above: Jack celebrating another successful feat after towing 65 boats with 6,500 pounds of Louisiana Pacific wood pulp at Lake Ashinoko in Japan. Daughter Yvonne, pictured front row, second from the left. Harry Merlo, CEO of Louisiana-Pacific Corporation, pictured behind and left of Jack. Below: Jack pulling 65 boats.

1980: Age 66. To kick off The Jack LaLanne Health Spa in Miami, Florida, Jack towed 10 boats containing 77 people in North Miami over a mile in less than an hour.

1984: Age 70. Handcuffed and feet shackled, fighting high winds and currents, Jack towed 70 people in 70 boats from the Queens Way bridge in Long Beach Harbor to the Queen Mary, a distance of 1.5 miles.

JACK LALANNE

1987: Age 73. After 45 years of becoming a chiropractor, Jack received the Patriarch Society of Chiropractors honor which he hung proudly in his house. It was a long road to hoe from the 1930's, 40's and 50's. He was made fun of, ridiculed, even called names like "nut", "quack", "crackpot" and "charlatan", but never once did it bother him. He persevered to what he believed in. Often Jack would comment, "Yesterday I was a nut and a crackpot, today I am authority!"

Patriarch Society of Chiropractors

Now Be It Known That

Jack LaLanne, L.P.J.

Having been in practice
_45_ years or more is herewith
Honored as a Patriarch

Dated this first day of January 19_87_
Patriarch Society of Chiropractors

William B. Price DC.
PRESIDENT

Emmett _R.C._
SECRETARY

2002: Age 88. Received a star on the Hollywood Walk of Fame. Left: Johnny Grant, Hollywood's honorary mayor and ceremony MC, Lou Ferrigno, Tom LaBonge, Jane Russell, Mickey Hargity, Keith Morrison and Russell Joyner. Right: Jack with his signature pose after receiving his Star on the Hollywood Walk of Fame. Below: Jack and Elaine with their children, Dan, Yvonne, and Jon.

2001: Age 87. Top: The Jack LaLanne Power Juicer was born with Tri-Star Products. Jack had juiced since he was 15 and used every type of juicer. Never would he sell a product he didn't believe in. This was a perfect fit. He sold millions of units worldwide. Bottom: Jack, Forbes Riley, TV Host, and Elaine ready for another infomercial for the Jack LaLanne Power Juicer.

IN THE FALL OF **2004**, just in time for Jack's 90th Birthday, ESPN Classic ran a 36 hour back-to-back marathon of his shows with various celebrities chiming in on the commercial breaks to express their good wishes. With no pre-screening announcements, the show became a hit all over again, 53 years after Jack's very first show! This page commemorates that event.

JACK LALANNE

LIVE YOUNG FOREVER

12 Steps to Optimum Health, Fitness & Longevity

FOREWORD BY ROBERT KENNEDY
New York Times bestselling author & renowned expert on health and fitness.

2009: Age 95. Jack wrote his last book, "Live Young Forever," with Robert Kennedy of Robert Kennedy Publishing. His last words on page 281 were, "I love sharing my world with the joy of my life, Elaine (LaLa). Our happiness has resulted from a commitment to loyalty, a common interest in keeping fit, and a healthy and fervent desire to help others." Although this book is no longer in print, Jack's philosophy embodies optimum health, fitness and longevity.

2014: Grand opening of The Jack LaLanne 5,000 square feet fitness center at the retro-themed Universal Cabana Beach Resort Hotel, next to the Universal Theme Park in Orlando, Florida.

Amid modern exercise equipment, you will find walls of Jack LaLanne artifacts, photos, trophies, jumpsuit, paddleboard, plus a television continuously playing his shows. The six-foot tall statue is a favorite photo stop for guests and visitors.

This is a replica of the longboard Jack paddled 32 miles, nine and half hours, non-stop, from the Farallon Islands to the San Francisco shore. This replica was made by his son, Jon Allen.

About the Authors

Elaine (Lala) LaLanne is a sparkling, vivacious, motivational TV personality and public speaker, known and loved by thousands for her spontaneity and personal life changing to people of all ages. She stimulates, motivates and educates!

As a television pioneer her career began in 1948 with a bread commercial in San Francisco. It then evolved to a co-host on a 90 minute ABC variety show where she met Jack LaLanne. Since then, Elaine has lit up screens all over America and has been an integral part of the Jack LaLanne television programs. In the 1980's she often toured the country promoting her books. With each book she vowed she would never write another one; she has written seven. Her last one, written with Jaime Brenkus, *"If you Want to Live Move- Putting the Boom Back into Boomers,"* was published in 2019.

Elaine has helped invigorate the Jack LaLanne Power Juicer infomercials and has

made appearances on countless television programs including The Today Show, The Early Show, Friends, Fox and Friends and Howard Stern. Her unique insight towards nutrition and staying in good physical condition is the reason. Today she keeps up to date and does many Zoom interviews and podcasts.

Pride and Discipline- The Legacy of Jack LaLanne with Greg Justice is the book she feels will give the public an insight to the fitness revolution and what he did to help it evolve. She is also hoping for a documentary and movie about Jack LaLanne so that his Legacy will live on.

At 96, Elaine hasn't slowed down. Her years of experience combined with her contemporary business savvy, she continues to provide an exclusive look into the inner character of Jack LaLanne. Elaine, known as "LaLa", looks young, acts young, and inspires people to be young at any age! With infectious excitement, she paints a picture of the "YOU" that you want to be.

Greg Justice is a best-selling author, speaker, and fitness entrepreneur and was inducted into the National Fitness Hall of Fame in 2017. He founded **AYC Health & Fitness**, Kansas City's Original Personal Training Center, in May 1986 and **Scriptor Publishing Group**.

He has been actively involved in the fitness industry for more than four decades as a club manager, owner, trainer, and corporate wellness supervisor. He has worked with athletes and non-athletes of all ages and physical abilities and served as a conditioning coach at the collegiate level. He worked with the Kansas City Chiefs, during the offseason, in the early 1980's, along with professional baseball, soccer and golf athletes.

Greg has authored or co-authored 30+ books including, *Treadside Manner: Confessions of a Serial Personal Trainer* and *Mind Over Head Chatter: The Psychology of Athletic Success*, and contributes to many international publications including, Men's Fitness, Women's Health, Prevention, Time, US News & World Report, New York Times, IDEA Fitness Journal, and Corporate Wellness Magazine.

Greg holds a master's degree in HPER (exercise science) (1986) and a bachelor's degree in Health & Physical Education (1983) from Morehead State University, Morehead, KY.

Greg is available for speaking engagements. You may contact Greg at info@gregjustice. com, or visit www.gregjustice.com for more information.

For more information on how Jack and I got together,
check out the last chapter of my book with Jaime Brenkus
"If You Want to Live MOVE - Putting the Boom Back into Boomers."

If you would like to see virtual home training videos
that Jack created and more information on Jack,
please visit _www.jacklalanne.com_.